Small business networking group goals

Larry E. Thompson

ABSTRACT

The purpose of this quantitative predictive research study, using network adjacency matrix analysis, content analysis, Kruskal-Wallis one-way analysis of variance by rank, and regression analysis, was to determine to what degree networking relationship tie-strength relate to referral exchange results (utility) among members of a referral exchange goal-directed networking group in New Hampshire. This study considered the association of relationship strength in the context and construct of goal-directed networking groups. Moreover, the nature of a dyad relationship, being strong, weak, or nonexistent, would have an association to the referral results people experience. The primary theories this study extends are Granovetter's (1973, 1983) and Burt's (1992) work on tie-strength, structural networking and relationship properties. The survey sample included 184 networking participants engaged in a goal-directed networking group in New Hampshire. The survey results suggest that no correlation exists between relationship tie-strength and referral exchange results.

TABLE OF CONTENTS

LIST OF TABLES

LIST OF FIGURES

CHAPTER 1: INTRODUCTION

Social networking as a productive and instrumental activity is ubiquitous, found throughout our contemporary business and social society, and receives much practical and research attention (Parkhe, Wasserman & Ralston, 2006). However, predominant network research attention is limited to functional mapping rather than determining purposeful use. While networks can be mapped within an organization or community, and used by the organizational actors and entrepreneurs to find information, resources, and access, it neither is accounted for nor measured in any tangible way (Badaracco, 2002). Networking must be conceptualized in the mind of the actor and executed in a rational way. Any prescription of a networking practice depends on the context, the situation, and the individual personality of the participant. For networking behavior and its possible value to an individual or organization to be realized, there must exist purposeful strategy and execution of action. It is human nature to be social, to network with one another, and important to any organizational construction (Parkhe et al., 2006). Yet the complexities of network structure and behavior are beyond any universal rule or law. If a leader or network practitioner socially engages with the wrong individuals in pursuit of a goal, opportunities may be lost. Therefore, leaders, organizations, and individuals must carefully select, activate, and manage their social network activities for results, or waste valuable time, energy, and money in the pursuit of any performance advantage.

Network relationships influence access to resources for those that use them, and may result in better information gathering and decision making (Jenssen & Koenig, 2002; McDonald & Westphal, 2003). Networking relationships that are strong increase the chance of access to resources and success for entrepreneurs (Jenssen & Koenig, 2002). Conversely, Chief Executive Officers (CEOs) who seek advice from only their strong network relationships or friends during strategic decision making may realize negative performance and unsuccessful strategic outcomes (McDonald & Westphal, 2003). Social networking activation is accompanied by complex interactions and behaviors that exist in the context of those network relations. Therefore, in some situations and contexts, certain network relationships are productive and advantageous, while other situations create limitations and risk. When network relationships are not productive to a mission, new and more productive means of success must be sought (Putnam, 2000). Which network an actor or organization is active in is as important as the relationships that form within those affiliations. Therefore, while networking and the development of social capital is important, the relationship ties produced within them, their strength, and their maintenance are also important. It is critical that scholars and practitioners of social networks consider relevant network relationship theory in combination with changing organizational social norms.

A predominantly accepted theory within the network literature is Mark Granovetter's (1973) analysis of the value of dyadic ties. His research suggests that weak-ties (within a network) contribute significantly to bridging small groups, thereby yielding networking results:

> the analysis of processes in interpersonal networks provides the most fruitful micro-macro bridge. In one way or another, it is through these networks that small-scale interaction becomes translated into large-scale patterns, and that these, in turn, feed back into small groups. (p. 1360)

Granovetter (1973) challenged the intuitive notion that strong-ties (close friends and kin) are more advantageous to yielding network results. He found that weak-ties (acquaintances) were more likely to bridge us to new information, resources, and unexpected opportunities (Putnam, 2000).

Granovetter's (1973) theory is both substantiated and challenged within the literature, but it remains an accepted and valuable theory within social capital research. Jenssen and Koenig (2002) found a contradiction to the weak-tie theory in the context of entrepreneurial activities for finding resources to support business growth. Their findings suggest that within certain contexts, strong-ties are more instrumental in realizing results. What is not determined is the usefulness of the weak-tie theory within other contexts. Granovetter's (1973) statement is that weak-tie interaction "in one way or another" (p. 1360) will translate into results. The present study examined if the weak-tie claim, in the unique contemporary context of new social structure groups, remains valid, and provides clarity about affiliation economic value within specific social capital networks. There is evidence that social norms have shifted within vocational communities and are affecting our social affiliations (Putnam, 2000). Specifically, people spend more time networking socially with the people they work with then those in their resident communities. These networking behaviors shifts are critical to leadership strategy, productivity, and performance results.

Membership in American professional and economic associations over the past four decades has doubled (Putnam, 2000). The American Bar Association's (ABA) membership was 34,134 in 1945. ABA membership is currently more than 410,000, representing the largest professional association (The Princeton Review, n.d.). The absolute numbers for professional affiliation membership of practicing physicians, lawyers, architects, accountants and others have grown ten-fold in the previous three decades while other civic, political and religious affiliations have decreased (Putnam, 2000).

> Thus, social capital in the shape of formal organizations of employees has not increased to offset the decline in political, civic, and religious organizations activity…Perhaps, however, a more subtle shift has occurred between residence-based and workplace-based networks, a shift from locational communities to vocational communities. (p. 85)

Because more people work outside the home and maintain friends within their professional networks, relationship ties are collected and managed differently. Rather than finding and maintaining friendship relationships at church and civic groups meetings, people develop and manage friendships at work.

Collection and management of relationships can be serendipitous or goal-directed (Kilduff & Tsai, 2006). Serendipitous network relations form haphazardly through interaction of any kind. Sitting on a board of directors or attending a Rotary International club event may produce a relationship for which some exchange of information and value may occur. While the purpose to participate in these activates to find information, resources, or business opportunities may be a selfish one, it is not a stated motivation of the actor or these organizations. Rotary International's mission is to improve society, not find business opportunities (Rotary International, n.d.). However, goal-directed network groups are established for achieving network-level goals (Kilduff & Tsai, 2006).

Goal-directedness is characterized by an organizing administrative role and a linking of the membership towards a stated network purpose. "[A] regional business network might organize around the goal of promoting member interaction and joint marketing. All relationships among business organizations in the network would be mobilized to achieve this goal" (Kilduff & Tsai, 2006, p. 89). Therefore, while a Rotary club certainly sponsors networking events, its members are engaging in serendipitous networking under the stated goals of altruistic community improvement. In more recent years, several goal-directed networking organizations have emerged and have found a place in the community to serve a specific networking purpose.

Business Networking International (BNI), a small-business goal-directed network referral organization, reports 84,000 members, 4,200 chapters, in 20 countries since its formation in the late 1980s (BNI-History of BNI, n.d.; Success Net, n.d.). This growth is expected to continue by adding one new chapter each day somewhere in the world. BNI's membership growth and success took place as traditional civic and community networks eroded (Putnam, 2000). While BNI and other similar external-organizational business development and goal-directed networks emerged, most network research remained within the organizational context. The present study will address goal-directed external networks, rather than intra-organizational or serendipitous networks.

Within any networking relationship, properties of exchange and reciprocity exist, as well as the ability to influence one another through a mutual expectation of value. "The way influence is acquired without formal authority is through the 'law of reciprocity' – the almost universal belief that people should be paid back for what they do, that one good (or bad) deed deserves another" (Cohan & Bradford, 1989, p. 7). This exchange of information, favors, actions, support, or resources is costly and time consuming. BNI members pay membership fees, meet for more than one hour each week, attend various BNI training programs, and meet outside of formal meetings with each other. Table 1 represents an approximate time commitment for a BNI member. In this one organization, almost 7 million hours are invested annually, or approximately $200 million in productive time. This does not include the time required to manage and organize group administration by the members, time commuting to events, or member investment in following up on the opportunities produced by their activities. BNI requires a substantial investment of time and money.

Table 1. *Approximate time commitment for a BNI member (BNI-History of BNI, n.d.).*

BNI yearly Individual member time commitment

Events	Frequency/year	Estimated time (hours)	Total Hours/year
Meetings	50	1.25	62.5
One-on-one meetings	12	1	12
Training	2	2	4
Mixers	1	2	2

Individual yearly commitment in hours	**80.5**
2006 BNI membership	84,000
Total membership invested hours	6,762,000
Man years	3,522
Estimate average yearly income ($60K/year)	$211,312,500

Considering the plethora of social and professional organizations leaders and professionals participate in for the purposes of accomplishing goals, either social or professional, the productive time investment of networking is vast. Therefore, ensuring that all organizational actors are considering and accounting for their time and energy towards network activities is important to productivity results. Is a network actor provided an advantage by associating with many weak relationships, or by creating stronger relationships with a target few? This research seeks to clarify this question in the context of contemporary goal-directed networking groups.

The purpose of the present quantitative correlation research study was to determine the relationship between goal-directed network membership relationship strength (tie-strength) and the goal-results these relationships yield. Tie-strength was determined through simple network analysis, creating a clear delineation between strong-, weak-, and null-tie affiliations among the goal-directed sample members (Scott, 2003). Goal-results were measured through analysis of referral development result records accumulated by the goal-directed organization. This analysis was performed on a sample of 184 BNI members in New Hampshire who are affiliated for the purposes of business development through relationship building and referral sharing. This study examined the usefulness of tie-strength in relation to business referral results, and the value of tie development in a goal-directed networks group.

The predictor variable in this quantitative study was tie-strength of the members within a goal-directed networking group, as determined using network adjacency matrix analysis to produce asymmetric data (Kilduff & Tsai, 2006). The criterion variable was the volume of referrals produced through member goal-directed behavior. The intervening variables included length of affiliation in the goal-directed group, frequency of meetings with members outside the group, frequency of attendance of training events hosted by the goal-directed organization, and time in profession.

Included in the remainder of this chapter is the problem statement, purpose statement, research question, hypotheses, background and theoretical framework, significance of the problem within leadership and organizational studies, and definitions, assumptions, limitations and delimitations of this research.

Statement of the Problem

Professional networking activities are vast, ubiquitous, growing, and receiving much research and professional attention (Parkhe et al., 2006). Networking relationships that leaders and their organizational actors develop may produce information and access (Jenssen & Koenig, 2002; McDonald & Westphal, 2003). Yet, while these networking efforts are mapped for linkage and direction, there is little accountability for tangible results (economic) or return on investment (Badaracco, 2002). In the past several decades, social relationships have shifted significantly from civic to professional communities (Putnam, 2000). The absolute number of professional affiliation memberships of accountants, lawyers, architects, physicians, and others has grown ten-fold in the past three decades. In addition, further globalization, technology access, an organizational team orientation, and the growth of small business support the likelihood of new networking methods being deployed and used (Parkhe et al., 2006). One goal-directed networking organization, Business Networking International (BNI), alone has grown to 84,000 members distributed within 20 countries, accounting for approximately $200 million annually in membership time investment (BNI-History of BNI, n.d.). The network literature emphasizes the value of developing weak and less dense network ties among network actors to provide bridges for finding network economic value (Granovetter, 1973; Ustuner & Godes, 2006). The literature also provides numerous examples of network mapping to substantiate the potential reach weak-ties can provide, yet few regarding the economic results of these weak-ties. Network actors provide much effort to reach the extended network. Therefore, knowing the tangible value of tie-strength relationships is important to the actor and sponsors of network organizations.

This research study examined the economic value of relationship tie development within a contemporary goal-directed networking organization. To fulfill this purpose, a quantitative research study surveyed members of a goal-directed business development networking group (BNI) in New Hampshire.

Background of the Problem

Contemporary network theory has a historical foundation in cultural anthropology, sociometry, psychology and graphic mathematics (Parkhe et al., 2006). This foundation parallels contemporary leadership and organizational challenges of developing appropriate corporate cultures, team development, motivation, influence and organizational structure. While the rational problem of how to relate for appropriate utility and economic value remains, the conditions that exist today are different and changing rapidly.

Before 1950, there existed two schools of organizational thought: administrative theory and social organization theory (Stern & Barley, 1996). Administrative theory focused on the firm's structure concerning internal operations. This was about internal efficiency based on engineering principles. Social organizational theory focused on relationships, power, influence, and what effect different properties have on one another. In 1938, Chester Barnard recognized the influences that both administrative and social thinking had on one another (Scott & Mitchell, 1987). Since then, the nature of work, the workforce, and the operating environment have changed. Work has shifted from physical labor to knowledge (Drucker, 1999). The very definition of production has changed in part to advances in capital (technology, tools and methods). Working harder is no longer as valued as working smarter. Figuring out smarter ways to compete has replaced diligence and stubbornness of process. Therefore, Taylorism (Frederick Taylor), Weberism (Max Weber), and other purely rational approaches to efficiency are outdated ideas based on outdated environmental realities. The contemporary focus is on the knowledge worker, a self-thinking and operating individual who holds newer operating principles.

Knowledge workers are effective and productive when they know their task, approach it with some level of autonomy, can learn from the activity and focus on quality rather than quantity (Drucker, 1999). They want to work for their organizations because they are valued for their knowledge and contribution. This requires an organizational structure and cultural environment that is more open, collaborative, and team oriented. Knowledge workers will not function productively and thrive under rational organizational principles. Therefore, the way organizations structure themselves must also change.

The way people organize to accomplish work has not changed while the behavioral expectations of workers have. Modern organizations are required to be more competitive because of "liberalization, privatization and globalization" resulting in a need for speed, flexibility, and agility (Pathak, 2005, p. 59). Parallel to these environmental changes, organizations have adopted new approaches to managing, including participatory team orientations (Erickson & Jacoby, 2003). Approximately 40% of firms with 50 employees or more report that they utilize self-directed teams to accomplish work (Osterman, 2000). Within larger establishments, the positive economic effects of these practices have been validated (Erickson & Jacoby, 2003). These forces require organizations to consider culture and employee values in the context of structure to release knowledge worker brainpower and energy. Drucker (1999) acknowledges the need to change how organizations govern:

> Within a fairly short period of time, we will face the problem of the governance of corporations again. We will have to redefine the purpose of the employee organization and of its management as both satisfying the legal owners (such as shareholders) and satisfying the owner of human capital that gives the organization its wealth-producing power--that is, satisfying the knowledge worker. (p. 95)

Therefore, the Protestant ethic organizational structures and governing models, and the behaviors to support them will no longer align to produce the results required to compete in a new world.

If governing models change, so must the structure. Non-linear and creative thinking requires connecting to many other people and organizations, and productively using the information they provide (Pathak, 2005). The challenge is the capacity of the organizations and their workers to find the best and fastest paths to the information they need to be successful. Formal and informal networks may provide that capacity, if people understand the utility of them. Understanding networks and the relationship potential within them will support the knowledge worker in a contemporary organizational environment. In addition, organizational contributors who consider the greater business community part of their relationship potential must maximize their knowledge work outside the formal organization. Therefore, relationships within a context, situation, and environment must align to affect productive behavior. The belief that the more people one knows, the better, regardless of circumstances, may lead to wasted time, effort, and resources.

Research can bridge theory and practice to make it practical and productive by considering circumstance and situation. The uniqueness of this study is the context of purpose and the construct of environment. The theoretical framework this study draws upon is general network theory, tie-strength theory, and structural hole theory (Burt, 1992; Granovetter, 1973, 1983). When theory combines with application, theory becomes useful. While social science theories are well established, there is value in comparing a theory's usefulness to real life contemporary situations.

Within the larger field of social networks, there exist two relevant fields of thought. Granovetter (1973, 1983) studied and documented his theory of tie-strength that has been generally accepted and rarely challenged (Jack, 2005). This theory illustrates the utility value of weak-tie attainment as a powerful tool for achieving new information within a network structure (Granovetter, 1973). Yet there is disagreement regarding the tangible value of tie-strength for varying purposes and contexts (Jack, 2005).

Burt (1992) drew upon general network theory and Granovetter's (1973, 1983) work to explore the structural network properties that are hidden within the network. More specifically, Burt (1992) determined that structural holes are disconnections within a network. According to Burt (1992), actors compete for network opportunities and access, and structural holes (disconnections) provide unrealized opportunities. Burt's

(1992) perspective of structural holes is that they are invisible and only evident by their absence. Holes represent the opportunity of the unknown. If bridged, the information is new and available. Therefore, finding a bridge is comparable to discovering an opportunity. By linking tie-strength (relationship) with finding a structural hole (referral opportunity), we find useful bridges within a network.

The properties of networking have received significant research attention recently because of its ubiquity within groups, firms, industry and society (Parkhe et al., 2006). While these concepts are not novel, and are intrinsic to the social aspects of humanity, the methods to yield maximum results from network activity are complex and contextual.

Within the literature, a relationship has been determined to exist among network activities, the organization, and personal growth (Lechner & Dowling, 2003). "The size of a firm's network early on – largely determined by the network size the entrepreneur brings into the company – strongly influences growth" (p. 2). However, little is known regarding the kind of dyad relationships formed to define this growth. The types of relationships within a network have been examined within specific contexts, but do not inform or prescribe relationship strategies for all contexts. Generalities about six degrees of separation, network structure, and other network properties remain interesting and important. Yet it is also important to understand and act upon dyad relationships within that network. Therefore, relationship dynamics within particular contexts are appropriate for refining network theory.

Drawing on network and tie-strength relationship literature, and applying these theories to the new contexts that are forming within new business social structures will add to the empirical data. Research on job attainment within institutional economic contexts is well documented (Granovetter, 1973). Research on macro firm results in the institutional setting has been documented (Lechner & Dowling, 2003). Small business results and the use of networking have been established (BarNir & Smith, 2002). Entrepreneurial network results suggest that both strong- and weak-tie networks are instrumental in success (Jack, 2005). For leaders, research has demonstrated that tie-strength matters when receiving advice and making important strategic decisions (McDonald & Westphal, 2003). Within new social contexts, professional affiliation for self-directed actors' networking in goal-specific networking groups provides a gap for this research.

Business Networking International (BNI) is a goal-directed network group that provides its members a networking context for finding opportunities. Member strategy is to develop a useful network for the purposes of finding direct referrals to other individuals that can bridge structural holes. BNI's stated purpose is to provide a supportive and structured system and environment (BNI: New Hampshire, n.d.):

> BNI provides a structured and supportive system of giving and receiving business. It does so by providing an environment in which you develop personal relationships with dozens of other qualified business professionals. By establishing this "formal" relationship with other people, you will have the opportunity to substantially increase your business. (¶ 5)

BNI's marketing positioning statement is "The business referral organization where givers gain" (BNI: New Hampshire, n.d., ¶ 1). BNI advocates the establishment of relationships through its procedures, and includes one-on-one meetings among members and establishing smaller teams where relationships can be leveraged for better referral development results. Therefore, this organization's primary methodology is to develop both weak- and strong-tie relationships among the members. This research examined the productive results of each relationship that was established.

Parkhe, Wasserman, and Ralston (2006) recognize the current macro shifts in organizational context, but believe future research will advance the understanding of how networks can improve business success. "[N]etwork theory development is at the cusp of an exciting new phase of advancement" (p. 560). However, if the network research merely analyzes complicated mathematical models and maps, understanding of organizational behavior may be missed, and how to apply successful methods will remain unknown.

> A network theory that accounts for the appearance and disappearance of structural holes--rather than how they can be used to advantage--and the consequent changes in interaction over time may provide us with a better understanding of how collective action is organized. (Salancik, 1995, p. 349)

Therefore, to advance the theoretical knowledge of networks, practical understanding of outcomes for these theories within time and space (contextual) are important. In addition, the utility and economic results derived from time and space may provide predictive application for similar goal-directed groups. This research did not yield a universal prescription for networking behavior, but it does inform leaders and professionals about utility and economic value based on a contemporary structure and the relationship practices of networking in a contemporary organizational situation.

Purpose of the Study

The purpose of this quantitative correlation research study was to determine to what degree networking relationship tie-strength affects referral exchange results (utility) among members of a referral exchange goal-directed networking group in New Hampshire. The predictor variable (tie-strength) was measured through network adjacency matrix analysis to determine weak-tie and strong-tie relationship dyads (Kilduff & Tsai, 2006). The criterion variable (results) was measured through content analysis of referral result data maintained by the group. These results determined the economic utility of each dyad relationship for correlation analysis. Intervening variables also collected included frequency of member one-on-one meetings outside the group's formal meeting, frequency of attendance of group training provided by the organization, time within profession, and length of group affiliation.

Significance of the Problem

The study of networks improves academic organizational research by focusing on macro rather than micro tendencies of organizational theory (Salancik, 1995). Used primarily as a tool to organize data about interactions, network analysis used alone does not allow scholars or practitioners to comprehend organizations completely. From a macro perspective, patterns of personal interaction "are associated with power, turnover, information flow, attitudes, promotion opportunities and social support" (p. 345). While it is valuable to understand these patterns and outcomes due to social connection, centrality, reach, and cliques, it is also important to understand the demand of obligation, constraint, strategic and economic value. Individual and organizational interactions can be both strategic and serendipitous, but to what extent and to what outcome? This research addressed outcome at an individual actor level within the context (purpose) and construct (structure and environment) established by a goal-directed group.

When network analyses (patterns) are combined with a context (structure) and relationship (interaction), analysts are less likely to describe any outcome or result as phenomena (Salancik, 1995). The context of a group may include roles, rules, and policies. However, relationships form within and around these contexts, never remaining proscribed or static. Naturally forming informal networks become relevant to both network and organizational theory. Parkhe, Wasserman and Ralston (2006) described the combination of structure and human interaction as player-structure duality, and suggested that network scholars benefit from an understanding of results derived from analysis of this duality.

> The structural designers of organizations, those who mandate reporting relationships or memo distribution list of access to databases, are much like architects who try to predict where the pedestrian traffic will be or should flow on a university campus. They lay their cement, install fences and other obstacles, but inevitably the flow of people and classes carve a bare spot in the grass where the sidewalks need to be. (Salancik, 1995, ¶ 8)

This research examined the bare spots (economic results) caused by combining context and construct of structure (goal-directed group) and relationship (tie-strength). To assume and prescribe the development of networks based on tie-strength or any other theory ignores the complexity of managing people in various situations.

To observe and document interactions provides a starting point to understanding our world. However, understanding how a structure can provide network actors an advantage, and to what degree, is important in improving network theory (Salancik, 1995). Network theory and its application hold practical value by informing people how to realize their goals.

> The implications [of understanding networks] extend far beyond networks
> – to students of management, strategy, organizational behavior, human
> resources management, entrepreneurship, alliances, knowledge and
> learning, and international business. Indeed, network theory has the
> potential to inform several contemporary issues, including the internet
> (Castells, 2001), "sleeper cells" in terrorist groups, epidemiologic studies
> of the spread of AIDS, and technology's impact on organizational
> structure and performance. (Brews & Tucci, 2004; Rodan & Galunics,
> 2004). (Parkhe et al., 2006, p. 567)

Understanding motives, member characteristics, selection of relationships, control, stability, and performance is informed by understanding our social structure and psychology that drive our macro society and micro behaviors. Therefore, any study that furthers network theory extends the understanding of how best to relate to one another in an evolving and complex world. Understanding the utility and value of network relationships allows for economic conservation and expansion of human capacity. This study addressed economic conservation and human capacity improvements regarding network activities. Competitive actors realize better results if they possess networks that are well structured and used effectively (Burt, 1992). Whether developed or inherited, actors who know how to use their networks and the connections they hold find more opportunities for success.

Network theory and application is reshaping organizational structure and architecture in a profound way, with the potential of global economic impact (Parkhe et al., 2006). The proliferation of autonomous and virtual companies complicates the competitive network properties by increasing the possible paths to opportunities, and requires an evaluation of how individuals and firms network. Complicating the overall social capital structures are proliferations and improvements in communications, transportation and computing. While these developments are intended to improve communication and access, they complicate our interaction methods and behaviors. Organizational structure is no longer limited to physical location or the traditional organizational pyramid. Therefore, leaders, business professionals, entrepreneurs, and any organizational actor may benefit from considering informal and currently undocumented ways to find access to people for results.

Because small businesses may lack financial capital and human resources, networks and the social capital may help to overcome size liabilities (BarNir & Smith, 2002). Success of a network relationship requires a propensity of an actor to network, develop ties within that network, and be perceived as useful to other network actors. Executives who develop and practice networking may create the proper conditions to acquire advantageous relationships, which create additional networking opportunities to extend their firm's goals. The tie-strength developed within an actor's network enhances cooperation towards enacting opportunities found, and further enhances partnerships. Furthermore, an actor's prestige within a network community provides credibility, utility, and wealth. Therefore, the network actor's ability to network, develop ties, and gain prestige works together to provide the momentum of success. This study examined a goal-directed group, which serves as a vehicle to accelerate propensity by providing a forum to facilitate networking activity. Within the goal-directed context, relationship tie-development holds the potential to provide opportunity. Understanding how successful opportunity finding is related to tie-strength informs leaders and professionals about the usefulness of goal-directed groups.

Entrepreneurial actions must convert limited resources (time, money, and people) into opportunities (Jack, 2005). To do this economically is a challenge. Leveraging others will provide access and opportunity and may transform a start-up firm into a thriving entity. "Therefore, nascent, embryonic and potential entrepreneurs should be aware of the advantages of using and developing appropriate networks" (p. 1256). Properly finding and leveraging the right network associates becomes important to short- and long-term success. In addition, firm leaders must direct activities appropriately to economically and successfully convert limited resources into value for their firms. The next section addresses this research's significance to the study and practice of leadership.

Significance of the Study to Leadership

A fundamental message of transformational leaders is that serving others is more important than serving oneself (Bass, 1990). True transformational leadership attempts to make positive change and fuse followers to a mission. Transformational change occurs when "one or more persons engage with others in such a way that leaders and followers raise one another to higher levels of motivation and morality" (Krishnan, 2001 p.126). It can raise the level of conduct and value for the betterment of all. In its pure form, it is unselfish, tapping into the needs of others and fulfilling those needs that are aligned with the vision of all involved. Transformational leadership requires a social perspective and commitment. This perspective can be large, including the whole society itself, or as small as every interaction between individuals. Therefore, leadership finds utility in every relationship formed.

Transformational leaders have a clear understanding that they cannot do it alone and leverage their followers to fulfill their mission. They embrace empowerment and trust as tools to execute change, and therefore require the ability to connect with people, trust them, and produce commitment. Bass (1999) believes these leaders "empower their followers by developing them into high involvement individuals and teams focused on quality, service, cost-effectiveness, and quantity of output of production" (p. 9). While a transactional leader may see this as loss of control, the transformational leader believes that a flatter organization is needed to create fundamental change (Bass, 1999). This implies that freedom of thought and all its value requires freedom of association. Therefore, networks and the relationships embedded within them provide value to a leader and the firm's mission.

A decade ago, it was normal for workers to go above expectations for their organization (Bass, 1999). As the workforce has become more professional and technical, and workers increased their need for their own self-esteem and confidence, it is unproductive to employ a theory x philosophy or utilize pure transactional leadership elements. Workers will remain unfulfilled as they desire to use their minds and ideas to help improve their organizations.

Transformational leadership refers to the leader moving the followers beyond immediate self-interest through idealized influence (charisma), inspiration, intellectual stimulation, or individualized considerations. It elevates the follower's level of maturity and ideals as well as concerns for achievement, self-actualization, and the well-being of others, the organization, and society. (Bass, 1999, p. 11)

To fulfill the transformational leadership ideal requires workers to be mature and individually successful, and seek self-actualization. Therefore, when transformational leadership is combined with modern knowledge workers, their relationship may be different than past leadership-worker relationships. These new leadership relationships are by definition deeper, mature, and mutually valuable. These transformational ideals extend beyond the traditional organization and into the external network of relationships.

Some workers have migrated to self-employment, franchising, outsource services, and home-based business because of job displacement or the desire to have a different professional lifestyle. This migration requires a transformational attitude based on strong relationship and influence skills. One way to motivate a prospect to purchase a service or influence an associate to provide support is through relationship. While the small entrepreneur's business model is important, moving associates and followers beyond self-interest can inspire and stimulate others to attain mutual goals (Bass, 1999). Therefore, transformational practices converge with knowledge worker goals and small business relationship practices. Networking and its inherent relationship value is a critical component to advancing the activities of these practices. The organizational leader or entrepreneur who embraces transformational philosophies will meet workers' and partners' requirement of trust and respect, and challenge all participants to do their best for those they support. Professional workers today require the transformational leadership style and competency to bring about the amount of change that modern business demands.

The information technology industry has several leaders of innovation and includes such companies as Intel and Microsoft. These companies are platform leaders and practice transformational leadership within their industry (Cusumano, 2002). They are successful not because they control everything; rather they influence their vendors, customers, and partners. They operate as conduits by leveraging their relationships, building trust, and recognizing respect for one another's abilities by developing freedom within their influence. While Microsoft may be criticized for trying to control its industry, it does embrace partnerships and a network of suppliers as critical components of its mission. If Microsoft's relationship with Intel disappeared, it could be risky to both firms' futures. Likewise, transformational leaders at any level within the organization must develop a network of people to connect with to leverage the advancement of their mission. In Cusumano's (2002) analysis, "wannabes" are companies that want to become platform leaders, yet fail to embrace the interrelationships of transformational competencies. Any leader or entrepreneur who does not embrace transformational competencies and develop a network of people to extend their efforts and influence may remain transactional, or only achieve Cusumano's wannabes status. To be transformational, network practitioners require skills of exchange, influence and reciprocity.

To exercise exchange, influence and reciprocity, a leader establishes and maintains varying formal and informal networks. Formal institutional networks are established through the role of the executive. Function, division, or company compartmentalizes inter-organizational networks. There is a mutual motivation among all inter-organizational actors to realize the company's vision and goals. Outside the organizational institution, leaders can have customers, partners, and industry affiliations that increase their network (Bass, 1990). Additionally, there exist informal networks that have no structure other than a reflection of the leader's professional and personal relationships (Cross & Prusak, 2002). These social networks allow the leader access to information, resources, and favors in order to be more effective. "Most corporations… treat informal networks as an invisible enemy--one that keeps decisions from being made and work from getting done" (Cross & Prusak, 2002, p. 104). However, these relationships allow an executive to influence and provide exchange beyond his or her formal control. Therefore, if Cross and Prusak are correct, organizational cultures that reject networks and do not allow them to flourish may be limiting the benefits these networks provide. The leader who can overcome the possible organizational norm that networks are harmful may have an advantage over peers and competitors who are less inclined to use a network to produce results.

Reciprocity and exchange properties are built into several management theories as tactics for leadership effectiveness and outcome. However, little empirical evidence exists that directly links reciprocity to both intrinsic and extrinsic leadership success. The literature has shown that the changing business environment is championing empowerment and decentralized power, which requires a workforce to behave more independently. This requires a shift to using influence without authority across individuals, functions, companies and industries. Therefore, social capital is of increasing importance for individuals to develop referent power and trust. These attributes are not written on an organizational chart, and each individual contributor is left to his or her own devices to develop and practice new relationship behaviors.

This study fills the gap in the literature by quantitatively studying reciprocity of referral results as a criterion variable of tie-strength. It is critical to our changing social world that the rules of networking activities be modified to improve individual and collective social and economic growth.

Nature of the Study

A quantitative predictive correlation research study was conducted to examine the relationship between network tie-strength relationship and referral development outcome for members of goal-directed networking groups in New Hampshire.

The predictor variable in this quantitative study was the tie-strength of the members within goal-directed networking groups, as determined using network adjacency matrix analysis to produce dyad asymmetric data (Kilduff & Tsai, 2006). The criterion variable was the volume of referrals produced through member goal-directed behavior. The intervening variables included length of affiliation in the goal-directed group, frequency of meetings with members outside the group, frequency of attendance of training events hosted by the goal-directed organization, and time in profession.

Predictive correlational research design is useful when the independent (predictor) variables and dependent (criterion) variable are measured over time (Creswell, 2002). In the present study, the predictor variable of tie-strength was established using asymmetric data analysis. The criterion of referral attained was collected over three months to determine the relationship between the variables. Correlational statistics measured the variables' relationship with one another.

Network analysis is the measurement of relational data (Scott, 2003). Relational data analysis measures contacts, ties, connections, and attachments that form a network link. To measure the relational tie-strength data in this study, affiliation-by-affiliation asymmetric data was collected through a roster-choice method. Roster-choice method identifies dyad relationship strength from a roster of names participants are provided, containing a complete list of a group's membership. This methodology was useful because it allowed respondents to directly identify and rank their affiliations, and indicate the intensity of their relationships. To measure relationship intensity, the concept of friend was utilized and is a consistent approach found within the network literature.

Varying definitions and situations can produce unique social constructs for social relations (Scott, 2003, p.53). Asking respondents to identify "friends" drew upon their conception of what a friend is. All people do not have the same definition for "friend" which may produce question wording artifacts rather than true answers. "Researchers are involved in a process of conceptual elaboration and model building, not simple process of collecting pre-formed data" (p. 54). However, friendship is considered the best single measure of tie-strength (Jenssen & Koenig, 2002). This research did not attempt to control respondents' conception by providing specific definitions. Rather, respondents were left to conclude their own emotional intensity among themselves. To further the reliability of this study, only people who chose each other as "friends" were considered a strong-relationship dyad.

The criterion of referral attainment was determined through content analysis of the data BNI maintains as part of the organization's standard procedures. BNI's current metrics collection methods include referral volume traded (given and received) among the membership. The "referral slips" (referral documentation) that pass between members were collected for the study's three month data frame to capture and report correlation between dyads.

Additional specific answers were collected to consider possible intervening variable effect. These intervening variables included length of affiliation in the goal-directed group, frequency of meetings with members outside the group, frequency of attendance of training events hosted by the goal-directed organization, and other related vocational questions.

The sample represents a true affiliation, independent of position, reputation or identity (Scott, 2003). General principles of sampling suggest drawing a representative sample from a network for homologous effect. Well-established mathematical rules exist to ensure reliability. However, in relational network analysis these rules do not apply because the resulting sample depends on the structure of the entire network. "There is no guarantee that the structure of this [a] sample network would bear any relationship to the structure of the corresponding partial network" (Scott, 2003, p.59). Because adjacency matrix analysis was completed for affiliation-by-affiliation, all affiliations were included in the survey. A 10% loss of data from a network population can result in significant loss of relational data needed for a network study (Scott, 2003). Therefore, analyzing network structural features is impossible with conventional research sample procedures. In this study, 10 whole groups were sampled in their entirety to provide a representative sample of the population, and 100% retention of entire target sample population within the 10 groups was unlikely. To satisfy the need for complete network population, all those from the target sample that did not participate were purged from the data. Therefore a complete network of interrelations was achieved.

While it is impractical to measure the entire BNI population of 84,000, or the hundreds of members in New Hampshire, it was possible to measure the entire population of several locations (10 entire groups). "If it is assumed that agents in a similar structural location in a network will have various social attributes in common, then it is possible to use survey data on the typical relations between agents with particular attributes as a way of estimating what structural location might exist in the network" (Scott, 2003, p. 61). Sampling ten 20-30 member groups in their entirety can yield relational data and suggest relationships and attributes for other groups utilizing a similar structure. Therefore, 10 entire BNI groups may represent the attributes of other BNI groups.

Empirical findings have supported the perspective of network relationships and the opportunities that exist within them (Ibarra, Kilduff & Tsai, 2005). More specifically, tie-strength, bridging, and structural holes are considered important towards economic transaction. Yet the context and constructs of these relationships vary among group goals and environments. Understanding correlation between variables that exist in varying contexts and constructs is important to predict strategies for varying situations. This research provides network relationship strategic insight for members of BNI, and may inform other goal-directed groups.

Research Questions

The purpose of the present quantitative correlation research study was to determine the relationship between goal-directed network membership relationship strength (tie-strength) and the goal-results these relationships yield. The literature supports the notion that tie-strength (weak or strong) does relate to network outcome in varying situations and environments. The present research considered the relationship of tie-strength in the context and construct of goal-directed networking groups. The following research question is reflective of this study's framework and purpose: Is there an association between relationship tie-strength and goal-directed outcomes for members of structured networking goal-directed organizations?

Hypotheses

This study sought to support null or alternative hypotheses. "Null hypothesis make a prediction that in the general population there is no relationship between variables or no difference between groups on measured variables" (Creswell, 2002, p, 143). "In a directional hypothesis, the researcher predicts the direction of relationship for measured variables in a population" (p. 143). The following are the hypotheses of this study:

Null 1: There is no relationship ($p>.05$) between tie-strength and referral outcome of members of a goal-directed networking group.

Alternative 1: There is a relationship ($p<.05$) between tie-strength and referral outcome for members of a goal-directed networking group.

Theoretical Framework

The theoretical frameworks this study drew upon were general network theory, tie-strength theory, and structural hole theory (Burt, 1992; Granovetter, 1973, 1983). To put these theories into context, this study examined network properties within a specific environment and structure that was designed for a specific strategy. Figure 1 illustrates the relationship of theory and related networking properties.

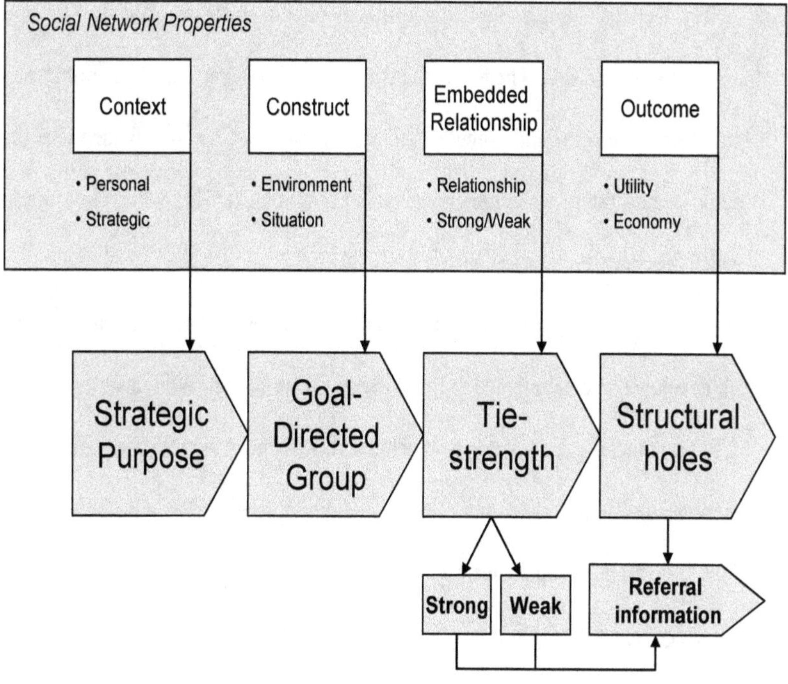

Figure 1. Social network property theories, content and construct.

The strategic purpose of a network actor provides the initial motivation for a

relationship and the behavior within it. This purpose can be operational or personal

(Ibarra & Hunter, 2007). For an outcome of any kind to occur, there is an initial purpose

to initiate an action. If an outcome of customer attainment is desired, a strategy may be

conceptualized and employed towards that outcome. For Rotary International members,

the stated outcome is to "[provide]s humanitarian service, [encourage]s high ethical

standards in all vocations, and [help]s build goodwill and peace in the world" (Rotary

International, n.d.). The strategy to achieve that purpose is to meet regularly, build a professional community, and draw on member talent to provide for community and society. Understanding and relating a strategy to outcome is important to a group's execution of a mission. Therefore, the structure developed to support the link between a group target outcome and execution strategy is important. This study identifies the initial purpose and strategy for achieving an outcome as context. This context informs structure, which this study defines as construct.

For an organization or group, structure provides the environmental constructs that are developed and maintained to make the group functional. While many groups may define an outcome and a strategy to achieve it, without an appropriate construct to support its existence, outcomes may be serendipitous rather than purposeful (Kilduff & Tsai, 2006). The group's construct will determine the network's trajectory or path. If that trajectory is purposeful, it is considered *goal-directed*. Conversely, if the trajectory is left unstructured, results are left to *serendipity*. A sound organizational goal is to provide a goal-directed trajectory to improve outcome. "Examples of network change driven primarily by goal-directedness include the trajectory of certain types of multilateral networks of cooperating firms as well as the trajectory of networking clubs" (Kilduff & Tsai, 2006, p. 89). Therefore, for a group to achieve its goal, it requires a purpose and a structure to support the trajectory of that purpose. Context and construct frame the purpose, environment, and situation in which relationships are embedded.

People are embedded in networks, and the relationships within them provide for the execution of network trajectory. Within the larger field of social networks theory, there are two relevant fields of thought. Granovetter (1973, 1983) studied and documented his theory of tie-strength that has been accepted and rarely challenged (Jack, 2005). This theory illustrates the utility value of weak-tie attainment as a powerful tool for achieving new information within a network structure (Granovetter, 1973). Yet there is disagreement regarding the tangible value of tie-strength for varying purposes and contexts (Jack, 2005).

Burt (1992) drew upon general network theory and Granovetter's (1973, 1983) work to explore the structural network properties that are hidden within a network. More specifically, structural holes are disconnections within a network (Burt, 1992). As actors compete for network opportunities and access, structural holes (disconnections) can provide opportunities. Burt's perspective of structural holes is that they are invisible and only evident by their absence. Holes represent the opportunity of the unknown. If holes are bridged, the information is new and subsequently available. Therefore, finding a bridge is comparable to discovering an opportunity. By linking tie-strength (relationship) with finding a structural hole (opportunity), we find useful bridges within a network. Understanding what types of relationship people have that assist them in finding opportunity that is economic was the purpose of this study.

A structure, within a context, provides for relationships to form that can produce desired outcomes. The literature supports weak-ties as having valuable reach properties for finding information (Granovetter, 1973, 1983). In addition, it is theorized that the primary method to reach opportunities is to bridge structural holes that are only discovered once they are bridged through these weak-ties (Burt, 1992). While these ideas have merit, and may be valid within specific context and construct, their usefulness may vary among groups.

To further frame the relationship dynamics within social networks, several micro relationship dyad properties were explored. Exchange, reciprocity, politics, trust, influence and persuasion all affect network trajectory and outcome. While these properties were not measured in this study, they have a motivational effect and assist in interpreting established theory and this study's results.

Definition of Terms

The following terms are germane to this study and are presented for clarification to the readers. The definitions provided are primarily from the network research and may have different meaning outside network research and this study's context.

Bridges are weak-tie dyadic social relationships that have the cohesive network power of connecting people and social networks to one another (Burt, 1992; Granovetter, 1973).

Centrality in a network represents the position an individual occupies if he or she holds many ties within the network, has the ability to reach other individuals inside or outside the network, or is physically centrally located for access to others (Kilduff & Tsai, 2006).

Cliques are subgroups (more than two individuals) within a network where all the individuals within the subgroup have ties to one another and no individual outside the clique has access to the entire clique (Kilduff & Tsai, 2006).

Density of a network represents the extent people are connected and know one another (Higgins & Kram, 2001). If people in one's network know one another well, the network is said to be dense. A dense network consists of strong relationships that connect actors together (Burt, 1992).

Dyad relationship represents a connection between two people within a network (Kilduff & Tsai, 2006; Scott, 2003).

Embeddedness represents the extent a network is nested within larger networks (Kilduff & Tsai, 2006).

Friendship represents a dyad attachment to another individual through mutual esteem and affection (Merriam-Webster, n.d.). In this research, a strong-tie relationship was considered a friendship. Tie-strength represents closeness based on emotional intensity within a relationship (Burt, 1992; Granovetter, 1973; Ibarra, 1997).

Goal-directed networks are characterized by providing an organizing administrative role and linking of a group membership towards a stated network purpose (Kilduff & Tsai, 2006).

Network cohesion (relationship tie-strength) represents familiarity and routine with a contact (Burt, 1992; Granovetter, 1973).

Range represents the extent of a network and the contact diversity it holds (Burt, 1983; Ibarra, 1997). It is "the number of different social systems the relationship stems from..." (Higgins & Kram, 2001, p. ¶ 26).

Serendipitous network relations form haphazardly through interaction of any kind and by any means (Kilduff & Tsai, 2006).

Social capital is the collection of relationships that hold the possibility of opportunity (Burt, 1992). Financial and human capital can be held in the form of money and resources, while social capital requires dyad relationships.

Structural holes are disconnections within a network structure (Burt, 1992). As actors compete for network opportunities and access, structural holes (disconnections within the network structure) can provide network bridging opportunities. Holes

represent the opportunity of access to other physical networks. If holes are bridged, the

information contained is new and subsequently available.

Tie-strength represents closeness based on emotional intensity within a

relationship (Burt, 1992; Granovetter, 1973; Ibarra, 1997). Ties that are close and binding

require more than a superficial emotional investment (Ibarra, 1997). Relationship strength

is the level of affection, frequency of interaction, and existence of reciprocity, mutuality,

interdependence and a motivation to help one another (Higgins & Kram, 2001).

Many of these definitions represent concepts used in network research and

analysis. These terms and concepts are not unique to this research and are used within

much of the network literature. Within the context of the present study, these terms are

considered to have the same meaning as presented within the literature. However, this

study's context presents several unique assumptions that are clarified in the next section.

Assumptions

This research held certain assumptions about procedures used and participant

perspective. To add clarity about this study these assumptions are identified. It was

assumed that the BNI context of strategic purpose (referral development) and the

construct of the goal-directed membership is shared across all BNI affiliations in New

Hampshire. Based on the clear and consistent BNI procedures that are the value of the

BNI franchise, it was also assumed that the BNI context of purpose and construct of

environment extend beyond the geographic scope of this study to all BNI organizations

that exist. It was an assumption of this research that individual BNI organizational

presidents would choose to participate and adhere to the research procedures. In addition, it was expected that 90% of the membership within each group would participate and that at least five strong-ties would be identified within each group.

It was an assumption that each BNI active member was engaged to improve his or her networking ability, referral results, and new business opportunity identification through participation within the organization in which they are affiliated. In addition, it was assumed that all members understand and adhere to BNI procedures.

It was an assumption that all participants provided an honest emotional response regarding their relationships within their BNI cohort. Within the literature, friendship is a well-established measure of relationship strength (Jenssen & Koenig, 2002). A friendship measurement represents closeness based on emotional intensity within a relationship (Burt, 1992; Granovetter, 1973; Ibarra, 1997). The assumption that friendship is a valid and acceptable measure in network research is consistent within the literature.

It was an assumption that the criterion variable of referral results were collected and kept with accuracy by each group.

These suppositions provide the reader with information about this study that is assumed and necessary to frame this research. These assumptions were monitored for contradiction during the course of this research. The next section describes this research study's limitations.

Limitations

Limitations represent aspects of research that cannot be controlled. A limitation of this study may be the ability to generalize the results beyond the BNI organization. While 184 members within 10 New Hampshire BNI groups participated, the type of businesses and professional practices outside BNI may be different from other similar networking organizations. BNI is unique because of its clear purpose, available training, and consistency of interaction. Therefore, other goal-directed groups assembled for different goal-directed purposes (i.e., community service) produce a different construct that may hold different results. However, this research may inform other groups about context and constructs that can produce better purposeful results.

The predictor variable for this study was strong-tie relationships among BNI members. It was an assumption that all participants would provide an honest emotional response regarding their friendships within their BNI cohort. Within the literature, friendship is a well-established measure of relationship strength (Jenssen & Koenig, 2002). A friendship measurement represents closeness based on emotional intensity within a relationship (Burt, 1992; Granovetter, 1973; Ibarra, 1997). While friendship is readily accepted within network research as a key indicator of relationship, each individual may have varying degrees of understanding and value for what constitutes a friendship. To control this limitation, mutual identification of friendship was a requirement for establishing a strong-tie friendship.

The criterion variable in this study was the referral results produced among the BNI members. The quality of these results (referrals) may vary. However, the context of the BNI meeting, the training members receive, and the organizational policy and procedures provide for some control of this possible limitation. A BNI member who has been trained (which is a requirement of membership) and is practiced in the group procedures understands the importance of referral quality. However, if members were new and had not attended training, this may have had an effect on the results. The survey qualified a member's BNI affiliation time. While it was expected that some BNI members were new to their group, all members are required to attend training in the first few months of their membership. The survey also inquired about participant's training attendance. These survey results were considered during data analysis to determine if result effectiveness was a valid limitation.

Possible limitations to this study's internal validity may be history, maturation, and mortality (Creswell, 2002, p. 325). History validity threats regard "Time passing between the beginning of the experiment and the end..." (p. 325). Maturation threats regard "Individuals develop or changing during the experiment..." (p. 325). Mortality threats represent attrition on a sample. These validity threats were controlled through the briefness of the experimental procedure. The predictor variable of relationship was measured at one time. The criterion variable of referral results was measured for a three-month period, prior to sampling tie-strength. While mortality did occur because of the different time frame each variable was measured, the procedure excluded people who dropped out of their groups. Therefore mortality was accounted for. It was probable that those who had been in the organization for less than three full months (newly joined the group) would be included. However, it was expected that 90% of the members included in this study would have more than three months of BNI experience. Therefore, any threat to internal validity was accounted for and controlled by excluding these risks from the sample data as they were identified during the study.

A possible limitation to this study may be interaction of history and treatment validity risk. This risk exists when generalizations cannot be made about past or future findings (Creswell, 2002). "One solution is to replicate the study at a later time rather than try to generalize results to other times" (p. 328). This study does not attempt to generalize about the past or future. Rather, this study represents the networking relationships that exist during a three-month period. Future research can replicate this study to reduce this risk.

Delimitations

This study confined itself to a target population within 10 BNI groups consisting of approximately 24 members within each group, or 239 BNI members. Of this target population, 184 members participated. Within this sample, the predictor variable of tie-relationships was measured and correlated to the criterion variable of referral results realized. All strong-tie relationships identified through the survey and resulting affiliation-by-affiliation asymmetric data were used in the analysis. However, if the individual relationships were not symmetrical within each goal-directed BNI group, the data was excluded from the study. Therefore, if someone named another as a friend, and that other person did not participate, that relationship was not included in this study. This ensured a complete and intact network. Weak-ties represented the total possible relationship of all included participants less the strong- and null-tie relationships identified through the survey. The next section summarizes the contents of this chapter.

Summary

Networking is a reality of the human experience and infused in all social constructs. Being social is human nature and important to any organizational construction (Parkhe at al., 2006). Network relationships influence access to resources for those who use them, and may result in better information gathering and decision-making (Jenssen & Koenig, 2002; McDonald & Westphal, 2003). Therefore, networking is important to individuals, leaders, organizations, and the execution of strategy. Varying situations, environments, individuals, and governance structures create advantages and limitations for network activity effectiveness. To maximize network activity results, productive methods to network must be found and applied (Putnam, 2000). Organizational paradigms have shifted in the past several decades to include more autonomous work and flatter organizational structures, resulting in new professional communities and affiliations (Putnam, 2000). Therefore, the environments and situations of networking activity have changed.

Predominant in the network literature is Granovetter's (1973) theory of the strength of weak dyadic ties. This theory emphasizes that weak-tie relationships provide an advantage to network participants, and are more valuable than close friends to produce tangible economic or utility value. It has been accepted within the literature that the number of people an individual knows is more important than the strength of those relationships. Subsequently, most of the network research focused on mapping these relationships rather than testing the value of relationship strength. This research considers the productive value of this theory in a contemporary entrepreneurial environment. Therefore, this study examined Granovetter's (1973) foundational theory's usefulness in the context of a goal-directed networking group. One such group is Business Networking International (BNI), whose goal-directed purpose is to produce productive economic value for its members through structured networking activities.

BNI, a small-business goal-directed network referral organization, reports 84,000 members, 4,200 chapters, in 20 countries since its formation in the late 1980s (BNI-History of BNI, n.d.; Success Net, n.d.). BNI's membership growth and success took place as traditional civic and community networks eroded (Putnam, 2000). The productive time investment in networking activities is vast. Therefore, ensuring that all organizational actors are considering and accounting for their time and energy towards network activities is important to practitioners and scholars. Is a network actor provided an advantage by associating with many weak relationships, or by creating stronger relationships with a target few? This research sought to clarify this question in the context of contemporary goal-directed networking groups.

The purpose of the present quantitative correlation research study was to determine the relationship between goal-directed network membership relationship strength (tie-strength) and the goal-results these relationships yield. Tie-strength was determined through simple network analysis, creating a clear delineation between strong-, weak-, and null-tie affiliations among the goal-directed sample members (Scott, 2003). Goal-results were measured through content analysis of result records accumulated by the goal-directed organization. This analysis was performed on a sample of 184 BNI members in New Hampshire who are affiliated for the purposes of business development through relationship building and referral sharing. This study examined the usefulness of tie-strength in relation to business referral results, and the value of tie-development in a goal-directed network group.

The predictor variable in this quantitative study was the tie-strength of the members within a goal-directed networking group, as determined using network adjacency matrix analysis to produce asymmetric data (Kilduff & Tsai, 2006). The criterion variable was the volume of referrals produced through member goal-directed behavior. The intervening variables include length of affiliation in the goal-directed group, frequency of meetings with members outside the group, frequency of attendance of training events hosted by the goal-directed organization, and time in profession.

The theoretical frameworks this study drew upon were general network theory, tie-strength theory, and structural hole theory (Burt, 1992; Granovetter, 1973, 1983). While these theories' primary purposes are to add insight to network structure, this research considered these foundational theories in the context of relationship and utility. To put these theories into context, this study examined these properties within a specific goal-directed networking environment that was designed for a specific strategy of network referral development. The next chapter (Chapter 2) reviews the literature that is pertinent to this study.

CHAPTER 2: LITERATURE REVIEW

The purpose of the present quantitative correlation research study was to determine the relationship between goal-directed network membership relationship strength (tie-strength) and the goal-results these relationships yield. Tie-strength was determined through simple network analysis, creating a clear delineation between strong-, weak-, and null-tie affiliations among the goal-directed sample members (Scott, 2003). Goal-results were measured through analysis of result records accumulated by the goal-directed organization. This analysis was performed on a sample of 184 Business Networking International (BNI) members in New Hampshire who are affiliated for the purposes of business development through relationship building and referral sharing. The study examined the usefulness of tie-strength in relation to business referral results, and the value of tie-development in a goal-directed networking group.

The predictor variable in this quantitative study was the tie-strength of the members within a goal-directed networking group, as determined using network adjacency matrix analysis to produce asymmetric data (Kilduff & Tsai, 2006). The criterion variable was the volume of referrals produced through member goal-directed behavior. The intervening variables included length of affiliation in the goal-directed group, frequency of meetings with members outside the group, frequency of attendance at training events hosted by the goal-directed organization, and time in profession.

This chapter provides a review of the theoretical and empirical research literature to frame and support the purpose of this study.

Documentation

A review of the most recent and relevant peer-reviewed articles and scholarly

books supporting the theoretical foundation, properties, and research was conducted. To

capture the most relevant and recent literature, several databases were searched and their

literature reviewed for this research study. Figure 2 illustrates the research map followed

for the study.

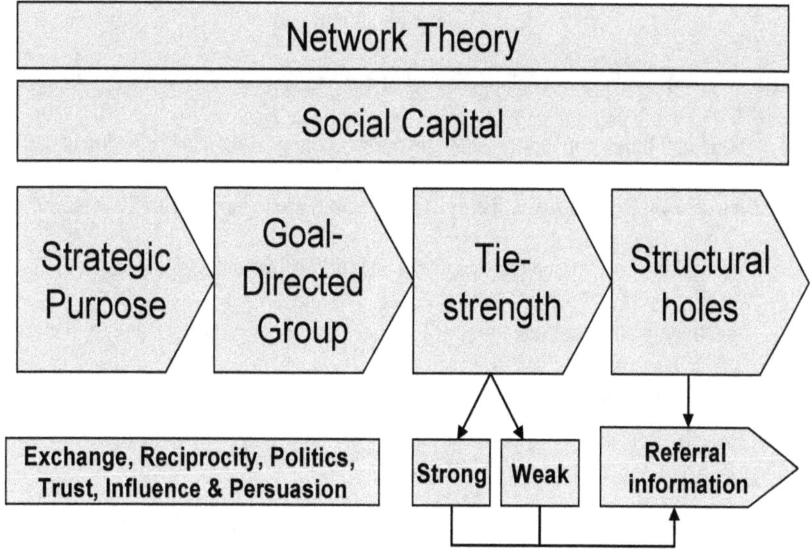

Figure 2. Literature map for the research study literature review.

Predominant within this review are several primary theories originated from

Granovetter's (1973, 1983) work on tie-strength and Burt's (1992) ideas regarding

structural holes. Much research emanated from these original ideas. However, much of

the contemporary literature focused on mapping network structures. In recent years, rather than validate or further test these theories, or place these theories within a contemporary context, researchers predominantly accepted these theories (Jack, 2005). Therefore, a gap in the literature exists, except for a few more recent studies on entrepreneurial effect for tie-strength. This research fills a gap in the literature with regard to the validity of the weak-tie theory Granovetter (1973) first proposed and places it in a contemporary business context and construct. The remainder of this chapter critically reviews this literature.

Literature Review

This chapter develops the definitions and themes of tie-strength relationships, structural holes, networking strategic purpose and goal-directed behavior as they relate to social capital and network theory. These themes are separated into five sections: (a) networking context and constructs, (b) network theory and social capital, (c) relationship tie-strength and structural holes, (d) exchange network properties, and (e) literature analysis and gaps.

Network Context and Constructs

This study identifies *context* as the initial purpose and strategy of any group embedded in a larger network for the purposes of achieving an outcome. This context informs structure. In this study, structure and properties are defined as *construct*. A method for managing context and construct of a networking group lies in its goal-directedness (Kilduff & Tsai, 2006). Network contexts, constructs, and goal-directedness have evolved to meet changing social properties.

There has been a social capital shift from locational communities to vocational communities (Putnam, 2000, p. 85). This parallels the competitive and organizational shifts, which require knowledge worker autonomy, flatter and empowered organizational management principles, competitive flexibility, agility and speed. Consequently, professional organizations are growing and professional relationships are changing. To support these changes, goal-directed networks provide professionals with alternative ways to realize productive network outcomes. Therefore, both the context and construct of networking social capital has evolved.

A networking context is a strategic purpose of an actor and provides the initial motivation for relationship and behavior within a network. This purpose can be operational or personal (Ibarra & Hunter, 2007). For an outcome of any kind to occur, there is an initial purpose to initiate an action. If a network outcome of customer attainment is desired, a strategy may be conceptualized and used towards that outcome. For Rotary International members, the stated outcome is to "[provide] humanitarian service, [encourage] high ethical standards in all vocations, and [help] build goodwill and peace in the world" (Rotary International, n.d.). This outcome, purpose, or strategy is the context of the group, and motivates its actors towards behaviors that fulfill their purpose. While Rotary International's stated purpose is not necessarily to network, members may use networking practices (i.e., weekly meetings) to advance the stated purpose. Therefore, while networking behaviors may be used, the goal-directed practice of networking is not shared among members and the organization's structure may not support networking activity. Consequently, networking may not be an efficient or maximized activity of the group. Subsequently, the group's purpose may not be realizing its full network utility or value to achieve its goals. All efforts, practices, procedures, rules, regulations, and norms must be structured to meet the needs of the organization's purpose. This subsequent structure is addressed in this study as construct.

For an organization or group, structure provides the environmental constructs that are developed and maintained to make a group functional. While many groups may define an outcome and a strategy to achieve it, without an appropriate construct (structure) to support its existence, outcomes may be serendipitous rather than purposeful (Kilduff & Tsai, 2006). The group's construct will determine the network's trajectory or path. If that trajectory is purposeful, it is considered *goal-directed*. Conversely, if the trajectory is left unstructured, results are left to *serendipity*.

Goal-directedness is characterized by providing an organizing administrative role and linking of the membership towards a stated network purpose. A goal-directed "regional business network might organize around the goal of promoting member interaction and joint marketing. All relationships among business organizations in the network would be mobilized to achieve this goal" (Kilduff & Tsai, 2006, p. 89). Goal-directed networks can provide faster access to information by being purposeful. Formal networks that create structure specifically for mining opportunities, creating relationships, and bridging structural holes may receive faster access to network value. A sound organizational goal would be to provide a goal-directed trajectory to improve outcome. "Examples of network change driven primarily by goal-directedness include the trajectory of certain types of multilateral networks of cooperating firms as well as the trajectory of networking clubs" (Kilduff & Tsai, 2006, p. 89). Therefore, for a group to achieve its goal, it requires a purpose and a structure to support the trajectory. Context and construct frame the purpose, environment, and situation in which relationships are embedded. The present study considers the value of the goal-directed structure that is present in BNI.

BNI, a small-business goal-directed network referral organization, reports 84,000 members, 4,200 chapters, in 20 countries since its formation in the late 1980s (BNI-History of BNI, n.d.; Success Net, n.d.). This growth is expected to continue by adding one new chapter each day somewhere in the world. BNI's membership growth and success took place as traditional civic and community networks eroded (Putnam, 2000). BNI's structure supports goal-directed behavior by providing a systematic and process-oriented forum for producing business opportunity referrals. While BNI and similar external-organizational business development and goal-directed networks emerged, most network research remained within the organizational context. The present study addressed goal-directed external networks, rather than intra-organizational or serendipitous networks. The next section provides a review of social capital and network theory.

Social Capital and Network Theory

The predictor variable in this study was the tie-strength between network actors within the context of BNI, a goal-directed network environment. These variables exist in a wider field of social capital and general network theory.

Network theory

Networks are fabrics of people woven together through connections, providing feedback, insight, information, resources, and support (Ibarra & Hunter, 2007). There are three interdependent constructs of networks: operational, personal, and strategic. Operational networks are those that assist an actor in accomplishing work. These can be people who interact together, including employees, bosses, and peers, and who coordinate activities that are part of a firm's or individual's technical role. Personal networks are those we relate with outside the operational capacity, who possess information and opportunities that are not available in the operational network. These networks hold the power of range, illustrated in the popular six degrees of separation analogy. Strategic networks are a collection of contacts that hold power to achieve goals. By employing strategic relationships, actors can access and influence the advancement of their causes. All three network constructs (operational, personal, and strategic) are important, can be developed and leveraged, and provide people, organizations, and leaders an advantage. These network relations exist within all social structures.

Social structure is composed of networks, ever developing and shifting, providing obstacles and opportunities. "The competitive arena has a social structure: players trusting certain others, obligated to support certain others, dependent on exchange with certain others, and so on" (Burt, 1992, p. 11). This network of relationships has structure and, depending on one's location within this structure, determines social and economic outcome.

Embedded network relationships that actors and firms hold have consequences (Kilduff & Tsai, 2006). Network tie structures are linked to job attainment, performance, and career success, and extend to health and mortality outcomes. Paul Revere and William Dawes both rode through Lexington Massachusetts to warn the colonials that the British were coming, yet Paul Revere is remembered for that historic outcome (Gladwell, 2000). In Gladwell's (2000) book *The Tipping Point*, he suggested that Revere knew where to go and with whom to share his message. It is also possible that he held different tie-relationships with that community's leaders. Revere had a more productive network, based on the results of his effort.

Network research examines the advantages and limitations relationship development has on gaining information and access to opportunities (McEvily & Zaheer, 1999). Formal and informal networks have structure and may produce behavior properties and tendencies. Understanding these properties and tendencies may provide a competitive advantage to individuals and firms.

While organizational theory focuses on the trees, network theory focuses on the forest and the organization of actions (Salancik, 1995). However, focusing merely on rational structure and its properties limits the understanding of what is going on within the cognitive and emotional connection between network actors. "Despite the apparent decisive effects that social contracts can have on the lives and well-being of individuals, much social science research has been silent concerning social influence" (Kilduff & Tsai, 2006, p. 3). While much research further defines the mechanical components of the network, and the macro results they yield within certain contexts, it is important to determine applications that modern organizations can use. "The potential application of the social network approach to organizations is, in our view, enormous" (Kilduff & Tsai, 2006, p. 4). Yet network theory and analysis can only provide a general understanding of rational structures that exist. To realize the potential utility of networks, the contexts that networks are embedded in are important. Since context can vary greatly, microanalysis of network outcomes, within a context, can inform specific people about specific network strategies.

Network research holds "emancipatory potential" by informing us of unobvious potentials of relationships and illuminating the inherent obstacles to social connectedness (Kilduff & Tsai, 2006, p. 23). Social realities that can be used for structuring social strategies emerge out of confusion. Strategies are important because of actors' capacity limitations. By determining strategy, a network actor can be more productive.

The volume of contacts an actor can hold, trade with, care for, and develop has physical limitations. In addition, the kind of relationships embedded in the network also can result in varying outcomes. To maximize return of investment (information in exchange for time and effort), maintaining a sparse network has the advantage of non-redundancy. "Size is a mixed blessing. More contacts can mean more exposure to valuable information, more likely early exposure, and more referrals. But increasing network size without considering diversity can cripple a network in significant ways" (Burt, 1992, p. 16-17). Therefore, network structure development and strategies can be managed to one's advantage, provide opportunities, and ultimately lead to tangible goal results. Understanding structural value within a context of an environment, goals, and practices that will provide a return on investment is helpful to a network actor.

Network analysis uses structural concepts and features to examine the components of network relations. Social capital, relationship ties, structural holes, and centrality detail primary network concepts and make them useful for network actors.

Social capital and informal networks

Organizations and their actors possess three forms of capital with which to compete: financial, human, and social (Burt, 1992). Social capital is the collection of relationships that hold the possibility of opportunity. Financial and human capital can be held (in the form of money and resources), while social capital requires dyad relationships. In addition, social capital is needed to transform financial and human capital into value. Therefore, while there may be money available to invest in products, and workers to manufacture them, without the means of connecting the products to a customer, no value can be created. Who we know is as important as what we know and what we control.

The network is a structure and conduit to others while social capital is the property needed to connect people within that conduit (Burt, 1992). Social capital is a healthy component that connects all individuals to each other as they strive to better themselves and their organizations. Social capital "is the 'gluey stuff' that binds individuals to groups, groups to organizations, citizens to societies" (Labonte, 1999, p. 431). Furthermore, there is more to this concept than affiliation. "The community as a whole will benefit by the cooperation of all its parts, while the individual will find in his association the advantages of the help, the sympathy, and fellowship of his neighbors" (Hanifan in Putnam, 2000, p. 19). The advantage can represent information, influence, and solidarity that people can attain based on the relationships they create (Bozionelos, 2003).

Social capital's primary benefits are access to information, timing of receiving that information, and referral development that enacts the access (Burt, 1997). In addition, it is an individual investment useful for finding and activating economic advantage (Kilduff & Tsai, 2006). Access to information can be problematic due to tendencies of selfish attention, uneven distributions of connections, and overload of information. A properly developed network can screen unimportant information and allow proper information through. It is also important that information distribution is timely. Knowing something important sooner rather than later provides an advantage with regard to a new opportunity.

Social capital within a network can provide legitimacy as well as reach (Burt, 1992). Referrals offered on one's behalf provide a better chance for opportunity information to travel through a bridge. A direct referral can be perceived as more legitimate than finding a name in a phone book. A job candidate who is offered a referral that is connected to a network of the hiring organization may have an advantage over other candidates.

Leaders and workers alike can achieve their goals through the relationships they develop, maintain, and put to use (Bozionelos, 2003). Achieving anything may not be possible in the absence of social capital and the networks it provides. The properties of social capital are *substitutability* and *appropriability*. Substitutability provides resources, direct access, information, and power. Appropriability allows the manipulation of purpose through friendship and provides support, access, information, feedback and exposure to other people of power. If these properties can be attained, there may be an inherent advantage that will lead to success. The literature also demonstrates this:

Gould and Penley (1984) found an association between a two-item measure of network participation and two indices of intrinsic career success, salary progression and plateauing. Canning (1988a, 1988b) reported a positive association between extrinsic career success and an unreported scale measure of utilization of informal intra-organizational network resources for career advice in a sample of middle managers. And Peluchette (1993) found a positive association between intrinsic career success and a two-item general measure of network

resources in a sample of academics. (Bozionelos, 2003, p. 44)

Therefore, there is a link between developing networks and both extrinsic (material) and

intrinsic (personal) reward. Reciprocity, being an outcome of social networks, may also

be associated with these rewards. As individuals develop, social capital can shape

personality as much as personality can have an effect on one's social capital (Bozionelos,

2003). Specifically, five personality traits (Five Factor Model) have been linked to social

capital development: extroversion, conscientiousness, openness, agreeableness, and

neuroticism. It may be important for network actors to possess certain personality traits to

achieve results, develop the necessary social capital, and ultimately use that capital for

the purposes of participating in reciprocity. As Bozionelos (2003) suggests, the

acceptance and use of reciprocity as a tactic can also shape one's personality.

It is important for organizational and network actors to invest in developing social

capital for attainment of referent power and increasing informal networks to enable them

to bargain in reciprocal relationships. Before social capital can be nurtured or used, weak

and strong relationships with people must exist, be bridged and managed, and solicit a

level of trust. The next section addresses relationship strength in the context of a network.

Tie-strength and Structural Holes

The predictor variable in this quantitative study was the tie-strength of the

members within a goal-directed networking group, as determined using network

adjacency matrix analysis to produce asymmetric data (Kilduff & Tsai, 2006). The

criterion variable was the volume of referrals produced through member goal-directed

behavior. A referral has potential to bridge member to an opportunity. This opportunity exists within a structural hole (Burt, 1992). What follows are the predominant theories on tie-strength and structural holes that shape the criterion and predictor variables of this study.

Tie-strength theory

While researching the link between job searches and network structure, Granovetter (1973) discovered that weak-tie relationships held valuable mobility properties (Burt, 1992). Within Granovetter's sample, he discovered that actors found their current job positions through distant rather than close contacts. People are embedded in social clusters that tend to know redundant information and discover new information at the same time. New information has to travel to social clusters, from other social clusters, through bridges. Bridges require dyadic relationships and network structures to exist. Relationships possess varying levels of strength and network structures possess varying levels of density. Therefore, tie-strength, density, and range are three properties within dyadic networks.

Tie-strength represents closeness based on emotional intensity within a dyad relationship (Burt, 1992; Granovetter, 1973; Ibarra, 1997). Dyad ties that are close and binding require more than a superficial emotional investment (Ibarra, 1997). Relationship strength is the level of affection, frequency of interaction, and existence of reciprocity, mutuality, interdependence and a motivation to help one another (Higgins & Kram, 2001). Weak-tie relationships provide bridges while strong-ties provide more psychosocial support (Higgins & Kram, 2001). The use of a tie-strength relationship strategy holds different value and results based on the need of an actor.

Density is the extent people are connected and know one another (Higgins &

Kram, 2001). If people in a network know one another well, the network is said to be

dense. A dense network consists of strong relationships that connect actors together

(Burt, 1992). Therefore, all people in that network receive the same information or

opportunity at the same time because the relationships are likely to share information

among one another more readily. Density results in redundancy of information and limits

range, and is generally considered less useful to a network actor who is trying to achieve

network range. Range represents the extent of a network and the contact diversity it holds

(Ibarra, 1997; Burt, 1983). Range is "the number of different social systems the

relationship stems from" (Higgins, Kram, 2001, p. ¶ 26).

Granovetter's (1973) strength of weak-tie theory suggests that bridges are

represented by weak-tie dyadic social relationships and have cohesive network power

(Burt, 1992; Granovetter, 1973). To illustrate his hypothesis, consider the relationship

links consisting of varying tie-strength depicted in Figure 3.

Ties & Bridges

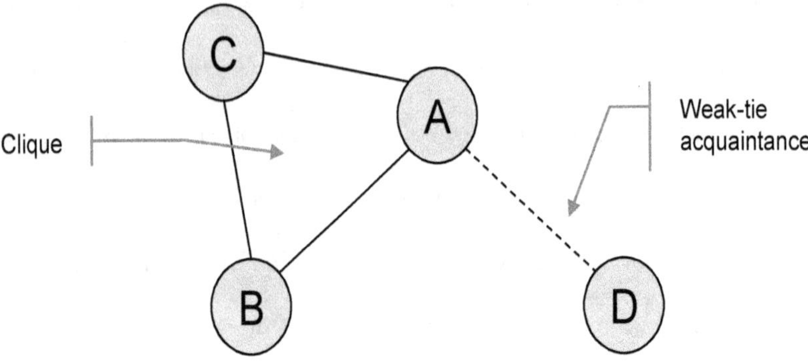

Figure 3. Ties and bridges (Granovetter, 1973).

In Figure 3, actors A, B, and C hold a strong-tie relationship with easy and credible access among them. When information reaches this relationship, they likely receive it at the same time, and it is shared readily among them. However, unless this clique has access to other relationships, information they receive is limited. If A and D have a weak-tie relationship, they will discover new information if they meet and actively share it. This new information is then shared within the ABC clique, and distributed to the clique's other strong relationships. The weak-tie between A and D serves as a bridge within the network and represents the only way new information can travel to a group.

Consequently, through this weak-tie bridge, information can defuse to any other bridge that extends from the network.

Diffusion through extended bridges may have distance limitations because of the time and effort required for information to travel. Therefore, Granovetter (1973) emphasizes the economic value of local bridges, those closest to the network link. The more local bridges an actor possesses, the more likely the inflow of new information. "The significance of weak-ties, then, would be that those which are local bridges create more, and shorter, paths. Any given tie may, hypothetically, be removed from a network" (p. 1365-1366). Understanding the utility and economics of each tie one possesses informs an actor how to maintain the most optimal network. "The contention here is that removal of the average weak-tie would do more 'damage' to transmission probabilities than would that of the average strong one" (p. 1366). Therefore, the weak-tie is more valuable to a network actor because of its transmission capability.

Granovetter concludes two major benefits for his weak-tie theory. Weak-ties provide utility because they provide longer range (reach) potential to distant information and offer economy due to shorter paths to direct information (breadth). If an actor has at least a few weak-ties, access to information is available, even if that information has to travel a longer path. Therefore, an actor will at least have reach distance to information from a contact's contact, and their subsequent contacts. A greater path distance can be traveled on weak-ties and their bridges, and are more valuable to the network actor than strong-ties. However, the utility value weak-tie information has depends on the length or range that information has to travel. The longer the network chain, the more effort must be expended within the network for information to be reached. The further out one extends the weak-tie chain, the less likely the information will be accurate, and the less motivated weak-ties will be to pass information along. Yet it is difficult to argue the structural logic of the reach utility potential weak-ties offer.

Granovetter's (1973) perspective is also that network actors who maintain more direct weak-ties (breadth) will have more direct and faster access to information and opportunity. The weak-tie theory of economic value for breadth is also logical from a structural perspective, but less so depending on the actual return on investment one receives based on the context and environment where exchange occurs. The assumption that more weak-ties will result in more information and opportunity has been validated, but only for employment seeking (Granovetter, 1973). Since employment practices are well established in the context of institutional structure, procedure, and organizational contexts, the environment and conditions are different from the context and organizational properties entrepreneurs and small business actors find themselves in. Granovetter (1973) also addressed the contextual component his theory depends on. "Treating only *strength* of ties ignores, for instance, all the important issues involving content. What is the relation between strength and degree of specialization or ties, or between strength and hierarchical structure?" (p. 1378). Since the context is different, the return on investment may be different for weak-tie breadth. Therefore, strong-ties may provide similar or more economic value than weak-ties offer in a goal-directed group constructed to share referrals and access.

The strategic uses of ties depend on the utility they offer. In a subsequent paper, Granovetter (1983) recognized that strong ties also hold utility and economic value.

Lest readers of SWT [*The Strength of Weak Ties*, 1973] and the present study

ditch all their close friends and set out to construct large networks of

acquaintances, I had better say that strong ties can also have value. Weak ties

provide people with access to information and resources beyond those available in

their own social circle; but strong ties have greater motivation to be of assistance

and are typically more easily available. I believe that these two facts do much to

explain when strong ties play a unique role. (p. 209)

Strong-ties are readily available, assuming they are developed and have motivation

properties. If an actor is advancing a service rather than a commodity, and requires a

personal referral to a target, strong-ties may hold more utility. Regardless of the network

reach potential of a network, without credible and trusting relationships between people,

and the willingness to provide a testimonial, having more strong relationships (rather than

weak relationships) may be a more important benefit.

Less empirical in Granovetter's (1973, 1983) research is the definition of tie-

strength. He conceptualizes four combined criteria for defining a strong-tie relationship:

time, intensity, intimacy, and reciprocity.

Most intuitive notions of "strength" of interpersonal tie should be satisfied by the

following definition: the strength of a tie is a (probably linear) combination of the

amount of time, the emotional intensity, the intimacy (mutual confiding), and the

reciprocal services which characterize the tie…Discussion of operational

measures of weights attached to each of the four elements is postponed to future

empirical studies. (1973, p. 1361)

The tie-strength definition criteria Granovetter (1973) employs is supported in his paper by several relationship theories rather than empirical evidence, making his interpretations plausible. Even so, preceding and subsequent research use variations of definitions. In a later study of job attainment, researchers used "friends" and "acquaintances" to separate strong from weak-ties (Granovetter, 1983, p, 206). In a study of business start-ups, the degree of friendship is measured based on close friend, friend, and acquaintance (Jenssen & Koenig, 2002). A study of tie-strength activation for entrepreneurs defined strength based on friends, friends of friends, family, and other characterizations (Jack, 2005). "[T]he problem with tie-strength is that it has never been given a precise conceptual definition" (p. 1254). The function of a tie, rather than time, intensity, intimacy, and reciprocity, becomes critical to defining tie-strength. It is likely that these properties matter, but to varying degrees in varying contexts.

A solution to determining tie-strength lies in the concept of mutual choice (Granovetter, 1973). Regardless of a tie-definition, if two people (a dyad) mutually choose one another as holding a certain relationship, a tie of some dimension exists. If two people are asked to list their friends, and both choose each other, it may be concluded they are friends. However, the definition of a friend can be different for two people. Yet if we provide the descriptive definition of a friend along with the question, tie-strength can be determined to some degree (Scott, 2003). In the present research, no definition was provided to the survey participants because of the intimate nature of the friendship concept. It is not the purpose of this study to conceive of a particular definition of friendship. Instead, the asymmetric approach was used to determine tie-strength for the study sample because mutual friendship is considered possessing a degree of friend

relationship. The asymmetric approach is illustrated in Figure 4.

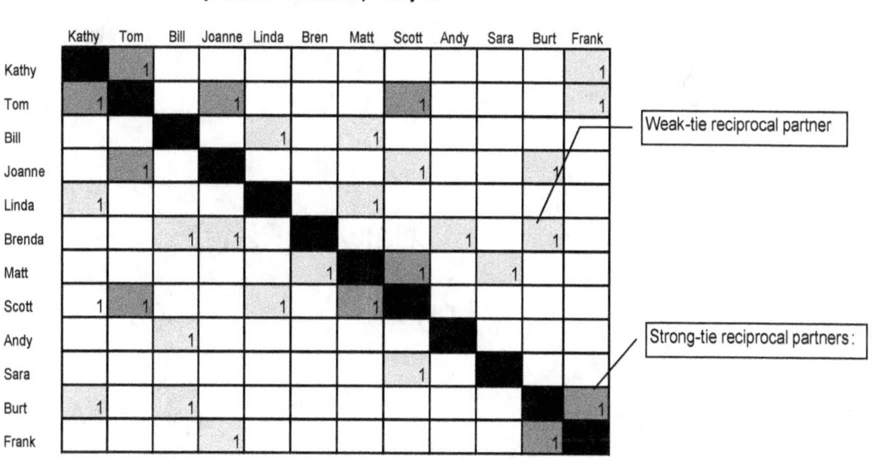

Figure 4. Asymmetric tie-strength analysis (Kilduff & Tsai, 2006).

In Figure 4, Tom and Kathy have chosen one another as having a friendship relation. In

this illustrative sample, five strong-ties are defined. Conversely, Linda has chosen Kathy,

yet Kathy has not reciprocated. It can be concluded that there is a relationship of some

kind, but it has not met the criteria of mutuality, and was considered a weak-tie for this

study's purpose. In this illustration, there are 20 weak-ties. Finally, Bill and Joanne have

not defined one another as having a relationship, and therefore no relationship can be said

to exist. While they may know one another, there is not a sufficient link between them to

have the network property advantages.

In the context of this study, understanding how tie-strength and density intersect provides a distinction between weak- and strong-tie strategies. In a study of mentoring networks, Higgins and Kram (2001) developed a network typology that is useful for conceptualizing the interrelationship between network structure and relationship properties. This typology is summarized in Figure 5.

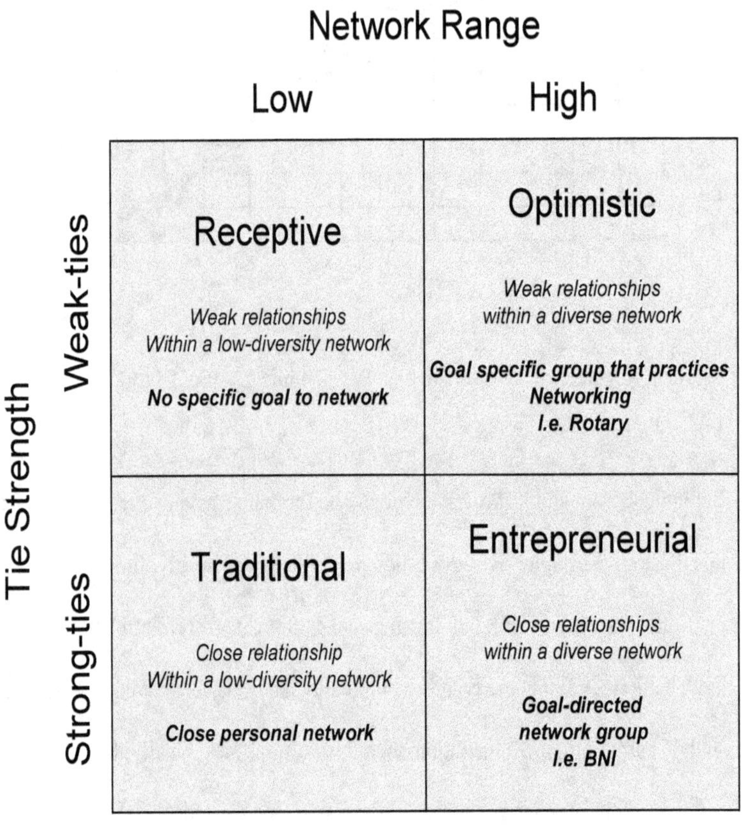

Figure 5. Network typology of range and tie-strength (Higgins & Kram, 2001, p 270).

In Granovetter's seminal work, *The Strength of Weak Ties* (1973), strong-ties are recognized as having valuable motivational properties that weak-ties lack. For entrepreneurs, their strong-ties are usually available and ready to help (Granovetter, 1983; Jack, 2005). However, this is limiting because strong-ties have low network range or do not bridge to other relationships (Granovetter, 1973, 1983). In addition, while strong-ties are valuable, if the ties lie outside the social system (an organization or club) the possibility of connection is less likely (Higgins & Kram, 2001). Therefore, it is important to an actor that both network range (diversity) and relationship (tie-strength) be considered when developing a network strategy that will yield utility and value.

It is likely that, even in a goal-directed group existing for the purpose of networking and referral sharing, several different tie-strength relationships exist. While Higgins and Kram's (2001) typology identifies certain strategies for network reach, not all dyads within a group will fall into one typology or another. BNI members may have access to range and diversity through their affiliation within a group, but how they manage the various relationships may be different. Likewise, a Rotarian (Rotary International member) may possess several strong-ties within his or her club, which may provide access to new opportunities. However, since the stated goal of a Rotarian is community service rather than referral sharing, no strong relationships may be needed to fulfill that mission. Conversely, BNI members may or may not need strong-ties to yield opportunities of referrals. What remains unanswered is which relationship (tie-strength) is likely to yield the best networking results from access and engagement within a group.

Therefore, for the purposes of this study, the entrepreneurial typology was examined that Higgins and Kram (2001) define.

Structural holes

Structural holes are disconnections within a network (Burt, 1992). As actors compete for network opportunities and access, structural holes (disconnections) can provide opportunities.

> A structural hole is a relationship of nonredundancy between two contacts. A hole is a buffer, like an insulator in an electric circuit. As a result of the hole between them, the two contacts provide network benefits that are in some degree additive rather than overlapping. (Burt, 1992, p. 18)

Burt's perspective of structural holes is that they are invisible and only evident by their absence. These structural network holes have relationship gaps that are unknown and can only be found through discovery. If an actor is not exploring the structural network that possesses these holes, the relationship gaps cant be bridged and network value will not be found. Holes represent the opportunity of the unknown. If holes are bridged, the information is new and subsequently available.

Considering a network as a web connected by individuals, any new relationship (or disconnection of a relationship) has an effect on the entire web. "Push here and someone over there moves" (Burt, 1992, p. 1). Depending on who is connected to whom, structural holes change and move. Therefore, knowledge and action within these holes provide entrepreneurs access, information, control, referrals and possible economic value.

Burt's (1992) structural hole theory is one of entrepreneurial freedom in a competitive environment. Structural holes are negotiated, not developed, held, or controlled. He argues that structural holes have little to do with player attributes or the results of activities. Rather, structural hole opportunities are attributes of player relations and the process of competition. "Competition is not about being a player with certain physical attributes; it is about securing productive relationships. Physical attributes are a correlate, not a cause of competitive success" (p. 4). Burt (1992) suggests that relationship development and the strength of these relationships within a social structure may be important for competing. Negotiating the relationship within a structure may be more important than how good one is at negotiating the network structure.

While relationship development is important, Burt (1992) is clear that people are the vehicles of action, not the source of it. The source of action, he argues, is the structure, connections, and holes. People, the players on a stage, are merely acting out improvisational communication within the structure provided by the director. The director's instructions are perceived as rule, while in fact the actor has freedom to change direction, or go to a different stage. Structure exists and people act within that structure, but can decide to look for new stages on which to perform, thereby deciding to exist and act upon another structure. Finding structural holes within the theatrical community can provide opportunity for the actor's art. Not recognizing that there are holes (opportunities) limits actors to the structure (stage) on which they find themselves.

Structural holes possess two conditions: structural equivalence (possession of similar contacts in a network) and cohesion (relationship strength) (Burt, 1997). A network actor can realize the opportunities that lie within structural holes if the possessed network is sparse rather than dense (Burt, 1992). A dense connection refers to close connections and relationship between people who know each other already. The assumption is that since they already know each other, they are likely to know each other's contacts, and have less available new information entering the dense structure. Therefore, fewer (if any) structural holes exist. A sparse connection will link to new contacts and information, and span structural holes that can provide new information and opportunity. Therefore, sparse connections offer non-redundant information (different and new). As an information monitoring device, dense networks are of little value. However, relationships may enact the density of a network by quickly finding bridges to new contacts that are continually developed by a group. Burt (1992) may be assuming that the dense network exists in isolation. Yet goal-directed groups are attempting to be active participants in networking activity and are likely to meet new people who can become new relationships. Burt's conclusion is that density is less valuable only if the network actors are purposely reaching out to new network actors.

Network cohesion (relationship tie-strength) represents familiarity and routine with a contact (Burt, 1992; Granovetter, 1973). The frequency of contact and emotional connection between people with strong-ties are likely to be redundant, lacking any structural hole opportunities. This assumption has been empirically tested with regard to job finding (Burt, 1992). Yet it is possible that a network that is structurally equivalent and has cohesion can extend itself to external networks if conditions (structure) and actions are modified. Therefore, if a context and structure is provided to facilitate structural equivalent actors with strong-tie relations to extend themselves into networks with structural holes, non-redundant information may exist to some degree. The BNI organization may represent such a structure and facilitated forum with the capability of finding structural holes.

As Figure 6 illustrates, a member possessing both strong redundant ties and weak non-redundant ties within the same affiliated group may have access to structural holes.

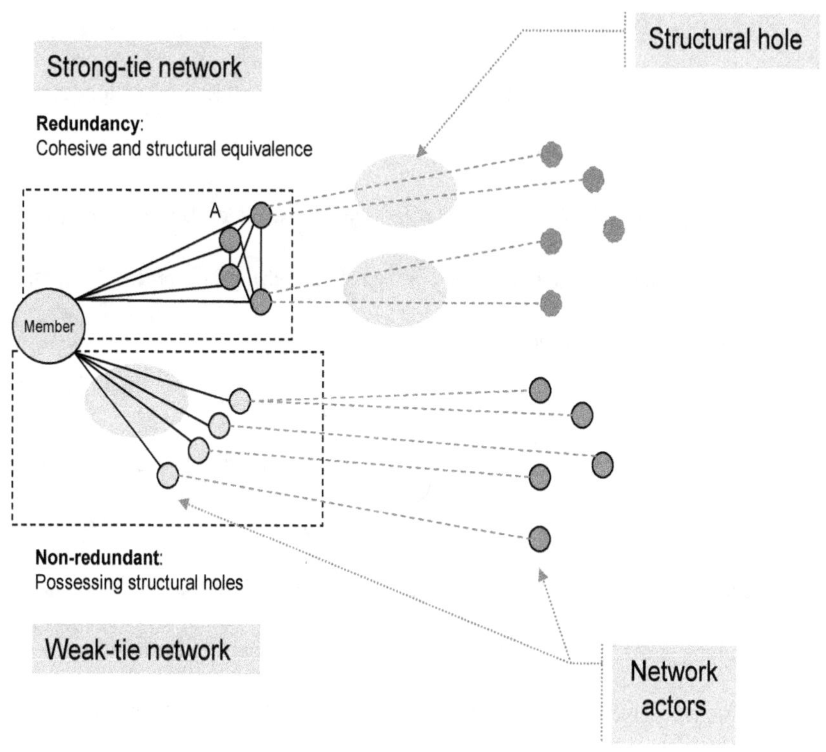

Figure 6. Structural hole reach based on relationship tie-strength.

Because BNI is goal-directed for the purpose of access to other people and networks outside the BNI affiliation, Burt's (1992) structural hole theory may not specifically apply. Burt addresses the advantages of an "optimally structured" environment for opportunity networking: "Players with a network optimally structured to provide these benefits [information access, timing and referrals] enjoy higher rates of return to their investment, because such players know about, and have a hand in, more rewarding opportunities" (p. 13). The access, timing, and referral value to BNI members based on tie-strength and structural hole properties cannot be assumed based on theory. BNI's goal-directed construct may provide an "optimal structure" that transcends or affects structural hole theory.

Within BNI's goal-directed context and construct, exchange properties exist. The next section discusses these properties, including exchange, reciprocity, politics, trust, influence and persuasion.

Network Exchange Properties

Social structure is composed of people acting within a network of relationships. Those relationships provide opportunities based on the interaction, perspectives and the activities of the actors. Social structure is composed of networks, ever developing and shifting, providing obstacles and opportunities. "The competitive arena has a social structure: players trusting certain others, obligated to support certain others, dependent on exchange with certain others, and so on" (Burt, 1992, p. 11). In BNI, the exchange of time, information, and mutual goals result in goal-directed exchange in the form of referrals. Several properties within the leadership and organizational literature provide insight into the obligation and acts of exchange. Reciprocity, politics, influence, persuasion, and trust are reviewed here to frame the actual behavior of trade within networking relationships.

Exchange

Exchange theory has a long theoretical history, which includes a scientific and rational perspective (Reynolds, & Skoro, 1996). Initially, exchange evolved from the Protestant ethic of extrinsic reward for a desired behavior (Wren, 1994). An actor would receive compensation (wage) for execution of management's desired task (job). Through the agrarian movement and the more recent industrial revolution, humans have changed the way they "produce and distribute output" (Reynolds & Skoro, 1996, p. 3). Specifically, more social relationships exist in our workplaces, which require re-examination of exchange. Therefore, a more modernistic and individual perspective is now championed within the literature. "If the value of a person or of an organization is based primarily on exchange, that encourages a set of social values and morals that cannot fully integrate the individual in an organization or group" (Reynolds & Skoro, 1996, p. 4). Pure exchange is not what people want, and will not produce diligence towards work. If leaders want workers to do their work voluntarily and in a social construct, the natural social desires and their associated tactics must be understood and championed. Reciprocity represents one of these innate desires. Exchange in the organizational context must include reciprocity, be allowed to flourish, and be used to advance an organization's opportunities. If not, organizations may not keep pace with the modern need to be agile and flexible.

Pure exchange may be harmful to our organizations (Reynolds & Skoro, 1996). It is considered good for workers to develop informal networks and use them for the organization's benefit. However, managers also want to be free from a reciprocal relationship with their employees. Maintaining a reciprocal relationship requires trust, consideration, and fairness. This requires leaders to make a shift from the predominant notion that exchange within a hierarchal structure provides them power and authority, to a more influence and reciprocal exchange perspective of their power. Therefore, contemporary organizations are in the middle of two organizational philosophies. Failure to recognize that pure exchange will not work with contemporary and future workers will produce ineffective leadership and strategies.

Reciprocity

Relationships within western business organizations can help an individual be successful (Vonhonacker, 2004). In eastern societies, however, relationships define the individual, ultimately advancing individual efforts. The Chinese called this *Guanxi*. "Guanxi networks entail reciprocity, obligation, and indebtedness among actors, as well as the aesthetic protocol that comes with cultivating these relationships" (Vonhonacker, 2004, p. 49). In the East, reciprocal relationships are more prominent in the business culture because of "constantly shifting political landscape, fragmented sources of authority, and the businesspersons resulting need to be an 'insider' at all levels of this hierarchical society" (p. 49). In the West, contemporary business has changed to include a diffusion of power, cross-functional teams, project management, partner synergies and empowerment. Therefore, the eastern ancient practice of Guanxi is a salient western contemporary reality.

The practice of reciprocity is not a short-term solution. It is a long-term strategy that requires the actors to collect help because it was provided to others at some point in the past (Baker, 2003). The emphasis is "on giving rather than getting…to [towards] building relationships. It is helping others without expecting reciprocity in return that –

paradoxically – invokes the power of reciprocity" (Baker, 2003, p. 13). Therefore, it is not necessarily a calculated activity. If it is recognized as calculated, it is less likely to be accepted as a trusting behavior. Reciprocity, while born from leadership utility, nurtured by social capital, and delivered through trust and power constructs, is useless if not authentically delivered. The act of reciprocity is successful through a balance of charisma, emotional intelligence, and long-term vision of the actor who uses it as a tool.

The law of reciprocity requires a balance of currency at some point in the future (Cohan, & Bradford, 1989). Currency represents inspiration, task, relationship, position, and personal related value as illustrated in Table 2.

Table 2. Commonly traded organizational currencies (Cohen, & Bradford, 1989, p. 11).

Commonly Traded Organizational Currencies

- **Inspiration Related**
  - Vision
  - Excellence
  - Moral/Ethical Correctness

- **Task Related**
  - Resources
  - Assistance
  - Cooperation

- **Relationship Related**
  - Acceptance/Inclusion
  - Personal support
  - Understanding

- **Position Related**
  - Advancement
  - Recognition
  - Visibility
  - Reputation
  - Importance/Insiderness
  - Network/Contacts

- **Personal Related**
  - Self-concept
  - Challenge/Learning
  - Ownership/Involvement
  - Gratitude

Reciprocal currencies are not found in any organizational chart, policy or procedure, and are not tracked formally by an organization or individual. It is a flexible currency and no accounting of payment is documented. It is the unwritten and sometimes unspoken agreement to act for another. The definition of a favor and its value to the actors is an approximation. To successfully participate, the actor must implicitly sense, or explicitly discuss any value, and the trade must be beneficial in some way to both individuals.

The currency of value available for trade exists between the actor's formal role and responsibility and the social capital they possess. Figure 7 illustrates this relationship.

Different Worlds of an Reciprocal Actor

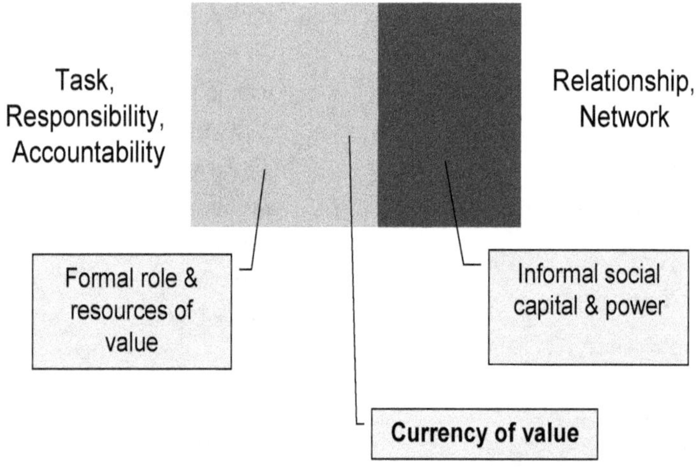

Figure 7. Currency of value available from the different worlds of reciprocal actors.

The overlapping value is the intersection between what actors need and what their social capital can offer. Therefore, it is important for the actors to understand one another's role and associated social capital.

Cohan and Bradford (1989) suggest four perspectives to consider during the act of reciprocity: See the target as an ally, know what the ally needs, understand what the ally values towards those needs, and understand exchange as a concept. In addition, the actor must seek a win-win situation now or at some point in the future. While it is important for an exchange to be authentic in purpose, there exists a need to understand and calculate what and how exchange will take place. Therefore, actors must be aware and actively strategize how to fulfill the needs of others. Most important, Cohan and Bradford (1989) suggest the importance of understanding exchange and its role. If exchange is not understood or embraced as a useful tool, it will not be enacted. Furthermore, if a reciprocal actor recognizes that a reciprocal target does not embrace a practice of reciprocity, no reciprocity will be purposely traded.

Regardless of availability of currency to be exchanged, several conditions must exist within that exchange. First, there must be a perceived relationship of timing of repayment (Sparrowe & Liden, 1997). For some actors, indefinite reciprocation is collected with no conditions of timing. For others, there may exist an explicit timeframe. There also exists a perceived equivalency of the currency. Again, this varies based on the actor's situation and needs. Finally, there must be a mutual interest to participate. This depends on the actor's self-interest or social desires (Werhane, 1994). For example, a trade of information may be helpful to an organization as a whole, but if the actor's interest is for him- or herself, an exchange may break down. If mutual interest does not exist, the reciprocation may be considered ingratiating or political behavior, and may result in a negative effect.

Organizational politics

Organizational politics has a negative connotation, both intuitively and within the literature (Lewis, 2002). The perspective of politics as an evil behavior is derived from how one defines politics and from the ability of a person to use it as a tool (Harrell-Cook, Ferris, & Dulebohn, 1999). In general, politics can be defined as the art of guiding and influencing in an effort to gain and control power (Merriam-Webster, 2004). Drory's (1993) definition of politics puts it in the context of the organizations: "informal organizational behavior designed to protect or enhance the self interest of individuals or groups when it is conflicting with the interests of others" (p. 60). The degree of action is relative to the size of the objective and the influence required. Actors practicing political behaviors can range from an individual within a small group to a CEO within a larger organization.

Interestingly, governmental politics is blatant and seen as a necessary practice to achieve an end. However, in business organizations some people view political actions as manipulative. In quantitative research, results have demonstrated that the perception of the use of political behavior is negative to those who do not possess the skills to use it (Harrell-Cook et al., 1999). Therefore, those with a negative perception are likely to have little control of their environment. Likewise, to achieve power "people engage [in politics]…to get power when it might not come naturally" (Lewis, 2002, p. 25). That is, they do not possess power to the degree they need in the natural course of events or are lacking in the facility of their natural abilities. Because of this, political behaviors may appear to be ingratiating. Yet, when political actions are executed elegantly, they may not even be recognized, resulting in a powerful tool for achieving results and change. Therefore, those who consider political behavior a negative value may be at a disadvantage within an organization or group that readily practices it. As organizations continue to champion empowerment and natural organizational systems, some knowledge workers will not thrive or will realize a social disadvantage.

Organizational systems have an inherent political element and may be a large part of normal human behavior. Pluralistic scholars believe conflict is natural and healthy in any organization and contributes to success in an ever-changing environment (Lewis, 2002). As in governmental politics, it is the debate and competition that lead to decisions that are ultimately helpful to the organization. Therefore, "because people are constantly competing for scarce resources, including higher-level jobs, the seeds of politics are built into our organizational systems" (Lewis, 2002, p. 29).

In a quantitative study of a large corporate change initiative, a CEO used politics as a valuable tool of a change process (Brooks, 1996). He created a culture of change through crafted events and methods. The organizational resistance was reduced by allowing failure to take hold, subsequently allowing his staff to realize that a change was necessary and inevitable. Then, he created new cultural symbols, provided new resources to support them, celebrated small accomplishments, developed strong relationship bonds, and practiced charismatic behaviors. The ultimate success was linked to the political tactics and behavior of the CEO. The subordinates embraced the methods as successful, fully recognizing that these methods were used. The staff accepted that their politically charged environment existed, began to model their CEO, and practiced politics themselves within their own business units. When people accept politics as a necessary and appropriate element of the system or culture, it become less divisive and more productive. Perhaps the CEO's tactics no longer were perceived as political once they were adopted by his staff as productive organizational behaviors.

In another quantitative study of leadership and political characteristics, several parallels were found, suggesting that transformational leadership and political characteristics are similar (Allen, Madison, Porter, Renwick & Mayes, 1979). Therefore, modern leadership and productive knowledge worker behavior is politics to some degree. In the study, eight personal characteristics of successful political actors were identified, of which most are considered necessary for successful transformational leadership. This begs the question: are effective leaders successful because of their use of politics, and do political behaviors result in advancement to higher leadership roles? Specifically, is reciprocity an important political behavior towards professional success?

It is disconcerting that politics, as a tool, is generally seen as negative for the organization, actors, and subjects. Negative aspects of political behavior can be career debilitating and potentially destructive; however, it is part of the human condition. "It may be claimed that OP [organizational politics] is an aspect of organizational behavior so deeply rooted in human nature and in the basic organizational setup that its negative implications can never be entirely eliminated" (Drory, 1993, p. 75). Knowledge and clear understanding of its successful application will help scholars and business professionals discuss this polarizing topic to the benefit of organizations and their leadership and contribute to the thinking about organizational effectiveness. In essence, BNI can be accused of enacting political behaviors. However, since all members accept the value of networking and its benefits, it is not recognized as politics.

Relationship development requires a level of mutual trust that is continually developed in the BNI membership through its context and construct.

Trust

Relationship building can take a rational marketing approach, which is only useful in the presence of trust (Blois, 1999). Many definitions of trust within the literature include the ideas of promise, confidence that the promise will be fulfilled, a sense of integrity, and an expectation of exchange (Schurr, & Ozanne, 1985). "Trust has been defined as the belief that a party's word or promise is reliable and that a party will fulfill his/her obligation in an exchange relationship" (p. 940). Therefore, in order for trust to exist, there must be a partner with which to exchange that trust.

The relationship by which people exchange trust can vary (Blois, 1999). If an actor knows someone well, and maintains a strong relationship with him or her, trust is continuously tested because of an established mutual reputation. In a strong relationship, if a promise is not kept or followed through on, a person may lose trust, however slightly. However, if a relationship is weak, actors are more likely to forgive someone based on the multiple variables that may have gotten in the way of the act being carried out. Another important consideration is whether trust is explicit or implicit. An implicit reciprocal promise not fulfilled can more easily be considered an oversight or misunderstanding of expectation. Therefore, the relationships within a network, being strong or weak, can offer different consequences with regards to trust. Strong links in a network are continually earning trust, while weaker links are given (gifted) trust. This forgiven trust supports Burt's (1992) assumptions regarding the network density being a disadvantage to bridging ties.

An argument can be made that many weak relationships are beneficial to leaders, perhaps as much as stronger relationships (McDonald & Westphal, 2003). In a weaker relationship, self-interest of the actors may remain higher. However, there always remains the possibility that in a weaker relationship, a participant with gifted trust may eventually "take our legitimate interest into account if such circumstances arise" (Blois, 1999, p. 204). Reciprocal actors accept a certain amount of vulnerability (gifted trust) to lessen complexities of the social arrangements made. If network actors collect many loose, uncomplicated, more forgiving relationships, they can anticipate that someone in the collected social network will fulfill an obligation that was once earned. Therefore, in order for reciprocal relationships to be more reliable in providing influence, actions, or favors, many relationships must be nurtured over an extended period. By ignoring or remaining inattentive to network relationships, a leader loses social capital, any established referent power or trust, and the ability to yield any benefit of potential reciprocal actions.

Influence and persuasion

Leadership and management requires motivating people to do things towards a goal. "[T]he essence of managerial work is an exercise in influence" (Kipnis, Schmidt, Swaffin-Smith, & Wilkinson, 1984). Therefore, influence is a component of the leadership definition. Why is it not considered a necessary component for all productive people within an organization?

Within the literature, several tactics have been researched with regard to influence, persuasion and organizational politics. All three subjects include reciprocity as a tactic. Influence tactics generally include rational persuasion, consultation, inspirational appeals, exchange, pressure, personal appeal, ingratiation, coalition and legitimating (Yukl, Kim, & Falbe, 1996). Exchange represents reciprocity in the literature and is seen as a successful influence tactic contingent on the situation and complexities of the relationship between the actors. The rest of the influence tactics can be utilized during the execution of influence with reciprocal targets. Just as a manager would influence an employee, so can a partner be influenced within a formal or informal network.

For a target to be influenced, several *content factors* must exist and be perceived (Yukl et al., 1996). Requests based on the use of influence must be perceived as feasible and any reward should be shared among the participants. The influencer must also be perceived as holding implicit, expert, or referent power. "Agent power in relation to the target person is another [a] determinant of influence outcome" (Yukl et al., 1996, p. 309). The power of the requester is important to the outcome of influence. In addition, a request must be perceived as important, the request must be interesting, and the targets must have some sense of the forecast of the results of their actions. These same content factors, to some extent, also exist within the act of reciprocity. If reciprocating participants perceive an equal exchange of these contact factors, reciprocity can continue. BNI context and construct may provide a relief to the power requirement within an influence relationship. Since the network activity is shared and respected among the group's members, relationship strength may provide a central causation of results.

Another important consideration of influence is which tactic to use for the purposes of motivating a target. A study conducted in 1984 found other factors that were important to influence outcome based on the requester's perspective (Kipnis et al., 1984). The selection of tactics used by the requester depended on the requester's relative power, the requester's objective for the influence, and the requester's expectation of compliance. Therefore, if the requester had more or less power, he or she would select a strategy felt to be useful. Situational considerations would also shape a request.

An early study created three profiles for agents of influence: shotgun managers, tacticians, and bystanders (Kipnis et al., 1984). Shotgun managers using many different tactics of influence reported many unfilled obligations, which suggested that they were inexperienced. Tacticians relied mostly on reason (rational appeal), yet mixed various other methods in varying combinations. Tacticians in this study reported satisfaction with their results. Bystanders used minimal influence tactics. They were either high or low in power. If their power was high, they had no need to influence. If low, they possibly did not even attempt to use influence tactics because they held no confidence that influence was useful to their efforts. This suggests that a position of power, or the informal power that leaders possess, is important to influence, reciprocal behaviors, and their outcomes. BNI members may represent tacticians because the BNI approach is purposeful and direct, allowing the BNI members to mix approaches based on the relationship situations.

In another study, Yukl, Kim, and Falbe (1996) determined that those with low power of any kind were most likely to use pressure as a tactic. They concluded that these agents did not know any better, and were at a loss for other available tactics. These findings suggest that it is critical for leaders and workers within networks to develop referent power in order to influence people within complex networks.

In the literature, persuasion was another construct that held reciprocity as an important tactic. There are six principles that can be used in framing persuasion: liking (establishing of similarities with people), reciprocity (people who give will gain in the long-term), social proof (peer power and testimonials), consistency (build commitment slowly over time), authority (expert power), and scarcity (exclusive information of results) (Cialdini, 2001). Reciprocity in this context illuminates the importance of relationships, gift giving, and praise as powerful tools to persuade. These principles are consistent with the influence literature. However, persuasion differs from influence by the power of the user. Persuasion can be attempted by anyone, regardless of station or relationship, and would require expert power rather than rank or referent power. BNI may represent a forum for persuasion as defined by Cialdini (2001). BNI provides a forum for relationship building, reciprocity, social proof, and consistency over time. In addition, BNI members may develop expert power and have exclusive information regarding referral results.

Regardless of power, reciprocity is a principle of persuasion and can be used by anyone capable of possessing the other principles. Therefore, a knowledge worker with no rank power, or referent power, could use his expertise, good reputation, and examples of good work to persuade others. In addition, he could practice reciprocation based on these attributes.

Gaps in the Literature

It is generally believed that networking activity provides for beneficial business outcomes (Jack, 2005). Yet much of the research theory is broad, while studies are primarily descriptive. An increased understanding and awareness of the tangible value associated with networking activities within specific context will improve understanding of networking application that is economical. "Economic activities need to take into account the context in which those activities are embedded" (BarNir & Smith, 2002).

Network theory considers the relationship between actors and systems (Parkhe et al., 2006). From this perspective, behaviors are constrained by the system in which they exist. Parkhe, Wasserman, and Ralston (2006) define this as player-structure duality.

> Consider carbon atoms, which may be structured in different ways. One arrangement yields graphite, the soft, greasy, black substance used in pencils. Another yields diamonds, the hardest known substance found in nature…These structural differences are certainly worthy of attention. Yet while the bonds between atoms are important, so are the atoms themselves…are they of carbon or hydrogen or nitrogen? The actors, and the interdependencies among them, are both crucial in determining the overall structure of the entity. (p. 561)

Many of the gaps in the literature exist within the context of player-structure duality. What may work for an intra-organizational environment with a specific purpose does not proscribe an approach within other contexts. While weak-ties may produce better advice for CEOs, they may be less useful for entrepreneurs searching for resources (McDonald & Westphal, 2003; Jack, 2005). What works for an existing multi-national firm may not be productive for a start-up (Jenssen & Koenig, 2002). Finally, what works for one person, group, organization, and industry may not be useful for another. Additional studies are needed to illuminate prescriptions and approaches for varying contexts. This study adds prescription clarity for goal-directed networking groups.

Parkhe, Wasserman, and Ralston (2006) examined recent network analysis literature to conclude several additional critiques. Network theory and analysis includes statistical analysis, sociometry, and graph theory. While important towards understanding structure, links, direction and reach, it remains inaccessible to many business scholars and organizational practitioners for practical use. Furthermore, integration of network theory with management research, including transactional economic accounting, may provide researchers and organizational actors a value accounting for network actions. The present study provides an accounting for networking activity through referral development of tie-strength properties.

Reciprocity maintains several dimensions that cut across many management and organizational theories. Most of these theories have been studied in detail, usually in sets of behaviors. Studies on influence revolve around the nine tactics as defined by Yukl, Kim, and Falbe (1996). Political tactics overlapped those of influence. Within the leadership literature, many tactics are described. However, few focused studies exist that validate reciprocity, especially over time and outside a sample study of students (Barbuto, Fritz, Marx, 2002).

Cohan and Bradford (1989) suggested that organizational actors have little understanding of the use of influence tactics. Yukl, Guinan, and Sottolano (1995) called for training around the power of influence. Sparrowe and Liden (1997) highlighted the relative lack of exchange used by organizational actors. Therefore, research is needed to illuminate the specific values of specific tactics available to organizational actors.

Bozionelos (2003) suggested that most research literature focuses only within organizations, not necessarily across companies or their external network. This study examined the use of reciprocity across external networks, not just those within the formal organization of the actor.

Another gap in the research is the nature of rewards people receive as a result of networking and influence. Bozionelos (2003) highlighted that only extrinsic rewards have been studied. In addition, Judge and Bretz (1994) noted that influence has been studied in relation to compensation, but not intrinsic satisfaction. Yukl and Tracy (1992) called for research to determine tactics that yielded compliance (results), not just commitment to the influence. The present study addressed these by examining referral rewards accumulated by the network actors based on friendship relationship strength.

The next section of this chapter summarizes the literature review and [transitions the reader to review this research study's methodology, design and appropriateness, examine how variables were objectified, and justify the research question and hypothesis.

Conclusion and Summary

This chapter developed and explored the definitions and themes of tie-strength relationships, structural holes, networking strategic purpose and goal-directed behavior as they relate to social capital and network theory. These themes were separated into five sections: (a) networking context and constructs, (b) network theory and social capital, (c), relationship tie-strength and structural holes (d) exchange network properties and (e) literature analysis and gaps. A review of the most recent and relevant peer reviewed articles and scholarly books supported the theoretical foundation, properties, and research conducted.

The purpose of the present quantitative correlation research study was to determine the relationship between goal-directed network membership relationship strength (tie-strength) and the goal-results these relationships yield. Tie-strength was determined through simple network analysis, creating a clear delineation between strong-, weak-, and null-tie affiliations among the goal-directed sample members (Scott, 2003). Goal-results were measured through analysis of result records accumulated by the goal-directed organization. This analysis was performed on a sample of 184 Business Networking International (BNI) members in New Hampshire who are affiliated for the purposes of business development through relationship building and referral sharing. The study examined the usefulness of tie-strength in relation to business referral results, and the value of tie development in a goal-directed networks group.

The predictor variable in this quantitative study was the tie-strength of the members within a goal-directed networking group, as determined through the use of network adjacency matrix analysis to produce asymmetric data (Kilduff & Tsai, 2006). The criterion variable was the volume of referrals produced through member goal-directed behavior. The intervening variables included length of affiliation in the goal-directed group, frequency of meetings with members outside the group, frequency of attendance of training events hosted by the goal-directed organization, and time in profession.

It is generally believed that networking activity provides beneficial business outcomes (Jack, 2005). Yet much of the research theory is broad and studies are primarily descriptive, focusing on network structure and mapping. In recent years, rather than validate or further test network theories, or place these theories within a contemporary context, researchers predominantly accept these theories (Jack, 2005). Therefore, a gap within the literature exists outside a few recent similar studies on entrepreneurial affect. This research fills a gap in the literature with regard to validity of the weak-tie theory Granovetter (1973) first proposed and places it in a contemporary business context and construct.

The next chapter illustrates and supports this research study's methodology, design and appropriateness, examines how variables were objectified, and justifies the research question and hypothesis. In addition, the subject sample frame, research procedures, instrument development, data collection, data analysis, validity and reliability are outlined.

CHAPTER 3: METHODOLOGY

The purpose of this quantitative predictive correlational research study was to examine the economic value of relationship-tie development within a contemporary goal-directed networking organization. To fulfill this purpose, members of a goal-directed business development networking group, BNI, in Manchester New Hampshire were surveyed to determine relationship strength among the members. The predictor variable (tie-strength) was measured through network adjacency matrix analysis to determine weak-tie and strong-tie relationship dyads (Kilduff & Tsai, 2006). Once dyad strength was determined, a content analysis of membership referral records was measured for correlation. Intervening variables were also measured, including frequency of member one-on-one meetings outside the group's formal meeting, frequency of membership meeting attendance, frequency of attendance at group training provided by the organization, and time within a dyad's profession.

This study is unique because it measured results for relationship strength in a context and construct designed to elicit referral results for all relationship strength development. Therefore, if strong relationship correlated to better results for reciprocating relationship actors, a case can be made for the value of strong-tie relationships for the purposes of dyad productive economic value.

This chapter illustrates and supports this research study's methodology, design and appropriateness, examines how variables are objectified, and justifies the research question and hypothesis. In addition, the subject sample frame, research procedures, instrument development, data collection, data analysis, validity and reliability are outlined. The next section supports the selection and application of the predictive correlation research design.

Research Design

A correlation is a statistical test of a pattern or tendency for two variables (Creswell, 2002). If two variables correlate together, they co-vary, and a prediction of outcome can be made from a score of another variable. A correlation of variables does not produce probable causation, but can "establish a likely cause-and-effect relationship between variables, rather than prove the relationship" (p. 139). Therefore, to determine possible causation, controlled research procedures isolate variables within a context to help explain if a relationship exists. In this research, the context of a goal-directed network offers a level of variable control.

Creswell (2002) outlines several criteria for determining appropriate statistical methodology for correlational research. These criteria were applied to determine proper research design. Creswell's criteria include the type of hypothesis to be tested, number of independent and dependent variables, existence of covariates, scale measures of the variables, and distribution expectations of results. Based on Creswell's (2002) criteria, non-parametric statistics were chosen for analysis in this study. Kruskal-Wallis one-way analysis of variance by rank was applied to understand the association between groups of relationship and referral results.

This study's hypothesis was based on a relationship between network dyads within 10 individual BNI groups. Several groups were tested for the purposes of achieving a statistically significant sample size for this study. However, these groups share the context of goal-directedness and are considered to be a larger group within the study population.

Creswell (2002) emphasizes the number of variables and type of measures required for a correlation approach. This study focused on one predictor variable (relationship-ties) and one criterion variable (referral results). This study's data represent ordinal measures for the predictor variable and integer measures for the criterion variable. Ordinal scores allowed participants an orderly measure to rank responses of friendship (Creswell, 2002). For the predictor variable of tie-strength, four ordinal measures are identified: (1) no relationship, (2), acquaintance, (3) friend, and (4) close friend. These measures were then combined into dyad relationships to produce the predictor variable data. For the criterion variable in this study, the amount of referrals traded among dyads was integer data. The statistical test used in this study to satisfy the research question and hypotheses is the Kruskal-Wallis one-way analysis of variance by rank, a nonparametric test used when data is ordinal (Sheskin, 2004).

Nonparametric statistics analyzes data that contain no assumption about population parameters or distribution (Sheskin, 2004). This study made no assumption regarding population distribution. However, the nature of the data collected suggested that the distribution of the population is non-normal (Sheskin, 2004).

Covariates represent the group of variables that confound the relationship of variables (Creswell, 2002). While any relationship is likely to be confounded by construct and context contingencies, these were controlled in this study through the construct and context of the goal-directed procedures for the BNI organization.

Appropriate for Desired Outcome

This study primarily compared two variables (tie-strength and results). Kruskal-Wallis one-way analysis of variance by rank is a nonparametric test used when data is ordinal (Sheskin, 2004). A *t*-test for independent samples was initially considered for this study's analysis of variables. However, a *t*-test is not appropriate because outliers have an effect on variability, subsequently affecting the impact on the sample means. The Kruskal-Wallis test reduces the impact of outliers by ranking the data. The Kruskal-Wallis one-way analysis of variance by rank was applied to all variable groups (tie-strength), and refined further to determine the statistical significance between strong- and weak-tie groups.

Predictor Variable

The predictor variable for this study was tie-strength, which was measured through network adjacency matrix analysis to determine weak-tie and strong-tie relationship dyads (Kilduff & Tsai, 2006).

Friendship is a primary measure of relationship and considered the best single measure of tie-strength (Jenssen & Koenig, 2002). Within the literature, tie-strength is an outcome of several elements. Tie-strength represents closeness based on emotional intensity within a relationship (Ibarra, 1997; Granovetter, 1973, Burt, 1992). Ties that are close and binding require more than a superficial emotional investment (Ibarra, 1997). Relationship strength is the level of affection, frequency of interaction, and existence of reciprocity, mutuality, interdependence and motivation to help one another (Higgins & Kram, 2002). In this study, frequency of interaction was controlled by the goal-directed group's procedure of weekly meetings for the purposes of interaction and consistent access to one another. Interdependence and motivation to share referrals is the goal-directed purpose. Therefore, the only variable that is not controlled or understood is the emotional intensity within each relationship.

Within the literature, variations of measuring tie-strength are minimal, and only vary based on categorical definitions of relationship. Granovetter (1973) utilized the terms close friends, kin, and acquaintances in describing relationships. Even so, preceding and subsequent research use variations of these definitions. In a later study of job attainment, Granovetter (1983) used friends and acquaintance to separate strong from weak-ties. In a study of business start-ups, the degree of friendship is measured based on close friend, friend, and acquaintance definitions (Jenssen & Koenig, 2002). A study of tie-strength activation for an entrepreneur defined relationship strength based on friends, friends of friends, family, and other characterizations (Jack, 2005). "[T]he problem with tie-strength is that it has never been given a precise conceptual definition" (p. 1254). The function of a tie, rather than time, intensity, intimacy, and reciprocity, becomes critical to defining tie-strength. It is likely that these properties matter, but to varying degrees in varying contexts.

In a more recent study seeking a correlation between tie-strength and citizenship behavior, the construct of friendship was also used (Bowler & Brass, 2006).

The strength of the friendship relationship between two actors was measured by asking employees to indicate whether they did not know the person (score 0), whether the person was an acquaintance (score 1), a friend (score 2), or a close friend (score 3). This resulted in a valued adjacency matrix, the friendship matrix, in which relationships are indicated by a number ranging from zero to three. The information was preserved in a directional matrix that reflects whether one, both, or neither of the parties indicated a friendship relationship. This information provided a directional indication of liking for each pair that was later used to calculate asymmetric social relationships. (p. 74)

This study utilized Bowler and Brass' (2006) definitions and procedures for determining tie-strength, which is well established and substantiated within the literature.

Network adjacency matrix is a relational data-sorting instrument used in social network analysis (Scott, 2003). It represents a direct comparison of mutual relations that are linked, and shows the actual ties among the network actors. Figure 8 represents this asymmetric approach to determine tie-strength.

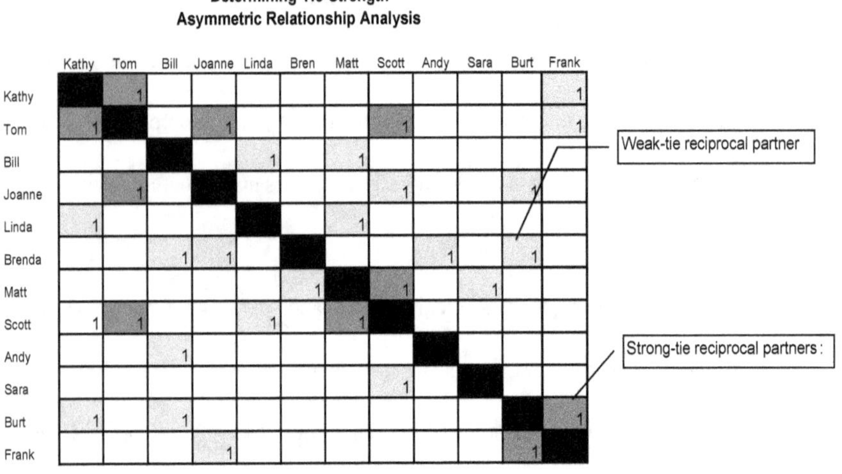

	Kathy	Tom	Bill	Joanne	Linda	Bren	Matt	Scott	Andy	Sara	Burt	Frank
Kathy		1										1
Tom	1			1				1				1
Bill					1		1					
Joanne		1						1			1	
Linda	1						1					
Brenda			1	1					1		1	
Matt						1		1		1		
Scott	1	1				1	1					
Andy			1									
Sara								1				
Burt	1		1									1
Frank				1							1	

Figure 8. Determining asymmetric tie-strength analysis (Kilduff & Tsai, 2006).

Determining tie-strength relies on the concept of mutual choice (Granovetter, 1973).

Regardless of a tie-definition, if two people (a dyad) mutually choose one another as

holding a certain relationship, a tie of some dimension exists. If two people are asked to

list their friends, and both choose each other, it is concluded they are friends. This tie

relationship can be collected and documented in an asymmetrical adjacency matrix.

Asymmetrical refers to the lack of symmetry in relations among the network actors

(Kilduff & Tsai, 2006). Therefore, if one actor chooses another as a friend, and the other

does not reciprocate that relationship, the data contained within a network matrix is

considered asymmetrical. Symmetry indicates a strong-tie among actors, and asymmetry

indicates a weak-tie relationship. This study's predictor variable was tie-strength, which

was identified by the symmetry or asymmetry of the data within an adjacent matrix.

In Figure 8, five strong-ties are defined. Tom and Kathy have chosen one another

as having a friendship relation. Conversely, Linda has chosen Kathy, yet Kathy has not

reciprocated. It can be concluded that there is a relationship of some kind, but it has not

met the criteria of mutuality, and is considered a weak-tie for our purposes. In Figure 8,

there are 20 weak-ties. Finally, Bill and Joanne have not defined one another as having a

relationship, therefore no relationship exists. While they may know one another, there is

no sufficient link between them to have network property advantages.

In this study, each group member was provided a list of all members within his or

her affiliated group with corresponding relationship choices to make. These relationship

choices are scored as: (1) no relationship, (2) acquaintance, (3) friend, or (4) close friend.

These scores were assembled on a network adjacency matrix to determine dyad tie-

strength data and then correlated to the criterion variable of referral results.

Criterion Variable

The criterion variable in this study was referral result. This information was maintained by each BNI group who meet and share network relationships. These results determined the value of each dyad's exchange relationship and were used for correlational analysis of the predictor variable of tie-strength. A primary activity during each weekly membership meeting is to pass referrals among members. This activity is the goal-directed purpose, the result of all other activities in which the group members participate.

Each meeting followed a well-defined process to enable and support the referral trading activity. Reminding members of the group's purpose and training updates during the meeting reinforces the goal-directed purpose. A standard agenda of each meeting, provided the control, consistency, and tangible purpose of referral trading activity. During each meeting, members are reminded of the purpose and overview of BNI, a network education moment is presented by the education coordinator of the group, business cards are collected and passed around the room for all to have access to, members have one minute to discuss their businesses, and reports are presented regarding referral trading results (BNI Directors Manual, Vol 2, 2005). In addition, each week one member presents his or her business in detail to remind the membership about what he or she does professionally, and what the best opportunities are for him or her to be provided through referrals. These activities are further scaffold by periodic outside BNI training seminars that are available to improve all aspects of performance of referral giving and receiving. One-on-one meetings between members outside the meeting assist relationship development for referral giving purposes. Referrals are the primary purpose for membership, meetings, and BNI relationships.

The process of trading referrals between members at a BNI meeting is accomplished through the exchange of *referral slips,* which contain predefined fields of information. A 4" by 5" referral slip (Form N. 0307) identifies who the referral is from, who it is to, and referral contact information for a prospect or target. It also contains the strength and nature of the target contact. These fields are well defined and supported by periodic training. Because a referral is defined differently than a lead, there is a requirement that the giver make contact with the target prospect so the referral is credible and the target will accept an invitation for interaction.

Each referral slip (Form No. 0307) contains three pages for distribution. The referral giver, receiver, and the BNI group vice president retain a copy. In this study, Form No. 0307 was collected and counted for each dyad to identify the referral results productivity for measurement. This analysis represented the criterion variable in this study.

BNI group vice presidents maintain a report on the exchange of referrals, attendance, and other metrics within their respective groups. This formal report of attendance and participation is the PALMS report (BNI Directors Manual, Vol 2, 2005). PALMS is an acronym for Present, Absent, Late, Medical and Substitute. While the title of this report emphasizes attendance, it also measures the referral participation which is considered a result of activity while in attendance. These metrics are collected for each active member, and include referrals given and received. This report does not provide the insight required for detail results among dyads because it does not report who gave a referral to whom. Therefore, the actual referral slips (Form No. 0307) were collected for the entire sample to account for each transaction. In this study, each sample group's referral slips were accounted for three months of referral activity, and matched for each dyad relationship.

Logical Sequence of Events

The sequence of research events followed a logical progression. The predictor variable of tie-strength was collected through a survey procedure during each group's active meeting. All surveys were completed in the month of September 2007. The criterion variable of referral results were collected for a period of three months, ending the week before the survey procedure began. Each BNI group's president was invited to participate a month prior to the study and was briefed on the study's purpose, risks, benefits, and process. No other BNI members were aware of this research prior to their participation on the day they were surveyed, and no other data was collected after the survey procedure ended. The day the survey was taken by each group's membership, all referral slips were collected for analysis by the researcher. Therefore, all data was collected for each group at the conclusion of each meeting.

Adequate Documentation to Replicate this Study

Because BNI is a well-established organization and follows consistent franchise procedures, the context and construct of this study can be replicated. The organizational purpose, philosophy, procedures and documentation are consistent across BNI. As long as a BNI organization follows well-established and documented protocol, this research can be replicated, expanded or adopted by future researchers. The only additional control required is to ensure that referral slips are collected for the period of study for the purposes of matching dyad results.

Appropriateness of Design

The purpose of the present quantitative correlation research study was to determine the relationship between goal-directed network membership relationship strength (tie-strength) and the goal-results these relationships yield. A correlation is a statistical test of a pattern or tendency for two variables (Creswell, 2002). If two variables correlate together, they co-vary, and a prediction of outcome can be made from a score of another variable. A correlation of variables does not produce probable causation, but can "establish a likely cause-and-effect relationship between variables, rather than prove the relationship" (p. 139). Therefore, to determine possible causation, controlled research procedures isolate variables within a context to help explain if a relationship exists. In this research, the context of a goal-directed network offers a level of variable control.

Creswell (2002) outlines several criteria for determining appropriate statistical methodology for correlational research. These criteria were applied to determine proper research design. Creswell's criteria include the type of hypothesis to be tested, number of independent and dependent variables, existence of covariates, scale measures of the variables, and distribution expectations of results. Based on Creswell's (2002) criteria, non-parametric statistics were chosen for analysis in this study.

The statistical test used in this study to satisfy the research question and hypothesis was the Kruskal-Wallis one-way analysis of variance by rank, a nonparametric test used when data is ordinal (Sheskin, 2004). The Kruskal-Wallis test reduces the impact of outliers by ranking the data. The Kruskal-Wallis one-way analysis of variance by rank was applied to all three variable groups (tie-strength), and refined

further to determine the statistical significance between strong- and weak-tie groups.

This research represents quasi-experimental design because it uses intact groups

that are available (Creswell, 2002). To reproduce a sample that replicates the exact BNI

organization's context and conditions is not possible. No treatment of the sample is

necessary. To apply treatment to the sample groups would negate the purpose of the

research because it would change the natural conditions that exist in the goal-directed

group under study. Therefore, quasi-experimental design is appropriate and critical to the

outcome of this study.

Research Questions

The purpose of the present quantitative correlation research study was to

determine the relationship between goal-directed network membership relationship

strength (tie-strength) and the goal-results (referrals) these relationships yield. The

literature supports the notion that tie-strength (weak or strong) does have an impact on

network outcome in varying situations and environments. The present research

considered the impact of relationship strength in the context and construct of goal-

directed networking groups. The following research question is reflective of this study's

framework and purpose: Is there an association between relationship tie-strength and

goal-directed outcomes for members of a structured networking organization?

Population

The population for this research was small and micro-businesses that utilize some

form of networking to advance their business results. This population is generally defined

as entrepreneurs, innovators and smaller enterprises consisting of business owners or small businesses representatives. According to the Small Business Administration's (SBA) Office of Advocacy, there are approximately 142,000 small businesses in New Hampshire (NH), of which 39,000 have fewer than 500 employees (SBA Office of Advocacy, n.d.). More significant is that 85,000 people are considered self-employed. This research may add insight to these self-employed workers and the small firm representatives' attempts to advance their products and services to market through referral generation and networking. Not all workers necessarily use networking as a productive marketing tool. Therefore, this research targeted the population who do use networking as a marketing tool.

Informed Consent

Participation in this study was voluntary and confidential for all research subjects. Any president of the ten individual BNI groups who did not want his membership to participate had the ability to opt out prior to the survey event. If a BNI leader agreed to allow the group membership to participate, during the procedure of survey delivery any individual members also could exclude themselves from the procedure.

Informed consent represents a dialogue between the investigator and the participants (Fylkesnes & Fylkesnes, 2003). Therefore, all participants were provided proper procedures for their involvement to maintain a clear understanding of this study and their involvement in it. Participants were presented with the research at the time the study survey was applied. Each participant was presented with a consent form and it was read aloud for clarity (Appendix A). The consent form included a description of the study, the information they were asked to provide, potential risks and benefits, indication that their participation was voluntary, reassurance that confidentiality would be maintained, and contact information for any additional inquiries they may have after they participated (Cone & Foster, 2002). The consent form specifically stated that their returning the completed survey to the researcher indicated their consent to participate. At any time during the procedure, any person was able to withdraw their participation.

The BNI organization had agreed to collaborate in this study and provided approval (Appendix B). They understood the nature of this research and agreed to provide access and documentation required for completion. Additionally, BNI management had authorized the researcher to conduct the survey within the confines of membership weekly meetings. The 10 groups surveyed met at 9 different locations, consisting of various restaurants, hotels and similar meeting places. BNI leaders rent these spaces and are responsible for the content of their meetings. Informed consent to use these meeting places was collected from the BNI leadership (Appendix C).

Sampling Frame

Business owners of smaller enterprises, their representatives, and self-employed workers who use networking as a marketing tool belong to clubs and organizations that provide some form of networking activity among their members. These groups include the Chamber of Commerce, Rotary International, industry associations, and networking clubs similar to BNI. Because most of these clubs have stated purposes other than pure networking, BNI represents the sample frame for this study because BNI's emphasis is on networking activity and referral generation. A sample frame "is a group of individuals with some common defined characteristics that the researcher can identify with a list of names" (Creswell, 2002, p. 163). BNI provided the accountable detail of members who are associated for the purposes of referral giving through relationship alignment. The BNI target population and sample frame represented the social construct and content

necessary for this study and provided a generalized link to small business networking

activity.

According to Creswell (2002), population and sample selection must consider

reducing coverage and sampling, measurement and non-response errors. BNI offered this

research the benefit of reducing these risks. The BNI population reduces coverage error

because complete lists are available and kept up to date weekly. The only coverage error

likely is sampling the wrong groups within this population.

All sources of this research's sample were drawn from BNI membership,

regardless of age, gender, socioeconomic status, or business classification. From the BNI

New Hampshire website, some general information was assessed and validated within the

study (BNI New Hampshire, n.d.). Table 3 indicates the BNI chapter membership counts

for this study's sample. This sample represented 10 chapters of the 35 total established

chapters in New Hampshire, representing Manchester, Derry, Nashua, and Concord New

Hampshire. This target sample contains 239 members, or 29% of the total New

Hampshire BNI membership.

Table 3. *Chapter and membership counts (BNI New Hampshire, n.d.)*

Chapter & Membership Counts

	Concord	Manchester	Nashua	Derry	Total
Chapter Number	3	3	2	2	10
Total Members	66	72	35	66	239
Average Membership/Chapter	22	24	18	33	24

Analysis of the 10 chapters studied indicated more than 11 occupational categories (BNI New Hampshire, n.d.). As presented in Table 4, professional services, financial services, and health and well-being professionals represent 56% of the target sample.

Table 4. *Occupational distribution of sample BNI members.*

	%
Professional Services	21.8
Health & Well-being	18.6
Financial Services	16.4
Facility/In-home Service	11.8
Contractor/Trade	8.6
Photo/Art Products & Services	5.9
Real Estate	5.5
Computer Services	3.2
Office Products	2.7
Education Services	1.4
Miscellaneous	4.1

Within these distributions, it was estimated that 47% of these business members were seeking business to business (B to B) and business to consumer (B to C) referrals. Another 37% were estimated to be seeking business to consumer (B to C) referrals only. Therefore, 84% of the members were seeking referrals to business or consumer relationships outside the group. Additionally, of this sample, it was estimated that only 28% of the members were representatives of a small firm, while 72% were representing their own business, either a small firm or micro business. Therefore, this sample was representative of the small business population of BNI and the extended New Hampshire small business population.

Because this study was network research and requires recognition of dyad relationships it was important that most of the membership within each group participate. However, if a member declined consent or did not participate, that data was purged from the data-set. In addition, any member not present the day of the survey was also excluded. Of the 10 BNI groups in the total group target sample, 184 members participated. It was estimated that a minimum of 5 strong-tie dyad relationships would result from analysis of each group measured. This would result in an overall strong-tie data result of approximately 50 (n=50). This study realized 323 strong-tie dyads within the data set.

Confidentiality

This research regarded network relationships and required participants to provide the names of the relationships they held with other members of their BNI network. Initial identification of participants was important to the nature of this network research. Anonymity and confidentiality was maintained by coding the data collected after all relationships were identified to the researcher. This study identified relationships that existed among the members and required matching up responses between participants to determine relationship dyads. Once these relationships were accounted for and matched to the criterion variable of referral results, data was coded for analysis. No participant names are revealed in any research documentation. All original documentation containing names are held by the researcher only and are locked in a safe. This documentation will be destroyed within 3 years of the completion of this study.

Geographic Location

Because BNI uses the same philosophies and practices across all groups, sampling error is minimized (Creswell, 2002). This study used convenience-sampling methods by selecting groups within the four largest cities within New Hampshire, and within close proximity to each other. In Manchester, Nashua, Derry, and Concord New Hampshire there were 12 well-established BNI groups that practice identical methods and are owned and operated by one owner-manager. Therefore, sampling error was reduced. One Manchester group was excluded from this study because the researcher maintains a relationship with several members of that group, and one withdrew before application. Therefore, 10 groups within these cities were used in this research.

Non-response errors within this sample population were reduced by obtaining study participation by each group's leadership prior to delivery of the survey instrument. If a group withdrew for any reason, another group within proximity of this metropolitan area was selected for inclusion. All participating group members could withdraw from participation on the day the survey was presented. Any data collected from those members excluded was purged from the data. The next section establishes the instrument used in this research.

Instrumentation

Friendship is a primary measure of relationship and considered the best single measure of tie-strength (Jenssen & Koenig, 2002). This study's predictor variable of tie-strength was measured through affiliation-by-affiliation asymmetric data analysis (Scott, 2003). This matrix methodology is applied prolifically in network research because it establishes reciprocal friendship relationships among members of a network. "This matrix…shows the actual relations or ties among the agents" (p. 40). As depicted in Appendix E, relationship data are presented in a rectangular matrix and indicates the reciprocal friendship relations through ego-centric measurement. To establish the necessary friendship relationships that exist within a network, the standard procedure in network analysis research utilizes a populated matrix format.

In a network correlation study of interpersonal citizenship behaviors, Bowler and Brass (2006) described how friendship relationship asymmetric data is collected.

Information for the friendship network was collected by using a list of employees similar to that used for the ICB [interpersonal citizenship behavior] network. The strength of the friendship relationship between two actors was measured by asking employees to indicate whether they did not know the person (scored 0), whether the person is an acquaintance (scored 1), a friend (scored 2), or a close friend (scored 3). This resulted in a valued adjacency matrix, the friendship matrix, in which relationships are indicated by a number ranging from zero to three. The information was preserved in a directional matrix that reflects whether one, both, or neither of the parties indicated a friendship relationship. This information provided a directional indication of liking for each pair that was later used to calculate asymmetric social relationships. (Bowler & Brass, 2006, p. 74)

Earlier studies also utilized this approach. Martin Kilduff (1992) researched friendship networks in relation to decision-making and described how relationship questioners resulted in the population of an asymmetric matrix.

Friendship was measured on the questionnaire by asking subjects to look carefully down a list of second-year MBAs and place checks next to the names of people they consider to be personal friends. The friendship data were arranged into a matrix of size 170 X 170 with cell entries of *0* or *1*. For example, a *1* in a cell formed by the intersection of Row 110 and Column 83 in the friendship matrix

> meant that Person 110 has nominated Person 83 as a personal friend. To make the
> matrix compatible with the bidding correlation matrix…the matrix was
> systematized using the rule that if either member of a pair nominated the other,
> then the pair was considered to be a friendship pair. (Kilduff, 1992, p. 172)

By combining Bowler and Brass' (2006) scoring approach with Kilduff's (1992) matrix approach, a clear dyad relationship matrix was constructed. The resulting tie-strength dyads established served the purposes of this study's predictor variable data for correlation to the criterion variable of referral results. Each BNI group studied received a list of their membership and was asked to report the strength of the relationship of each member. Appendix D represents the questionnaire developed for this purpose.

An additional intervening data inquiry was added at the end of each list for the subjects to answer. These intervening questions provided insight into the possible maturity of individual network activity and indicated use of prescribed BNI principles of goal-directed activity.

Network relationship research may still be considered a new phenomenon and worthy of quantitative research attention (Jack, 2005). However, the present research has the goal-directed purpose of the BNI control group. BNI offers a specific environment to test qualitatively and quantitatively the established tie-strength theory. Because questions can be narrowed to specific variables within a specific context, a quantitative research method enables the specific predictor variable of tie-strength to be directly correlated to the group's results (Creswell, 2002). The BNI experience is common among its members and the network purposes are more clearly understood than those in other less organized groups. In addition, the BNI culture is shared through the group's procedures and experiences. Therefore, a quantitative method allows this research to specifically isolate variables.

If the results of this study determine that strong-tie relationships are more valuable towards results, future qualitative analysis may explore the phenomenon of individual experiences in referral sharing. Jack's (2005) qualitative study of resource use in relation to tie-strength is justifiable because of reliability issues within network research. Her study attempted to explore and isolate variables. This study, within the BNI and goal-directed context, provided the variables needed for a positive research approach.

In behavioral science an important criteria for use of any instrument is that reliable data is produced (Cone & Foster, 2002). "Reliability means that individual scores from an instrument should be nearly the same or stable on repeated administration of the instrument, they should be free from source measurement errors, and they should be consistent" (Creswell, 2002, p. 180). To ensure reliability, instrument questions must be clear, procedures used must be consistent, standardized subjects must be able to understand the questions, and the procedure must be comfortable for the participants. This research used affiliation-by-affiliation asymmetric data analysis produced from the friendship list procedure described and used by Bowler and Brass' (2006) and Kilduff (1992). In addition, this simple network analysis of friendship measurement is described by Burt (1992), Granovetter (1973), and procedurally described by Scott (2003). Therefore, the well-established method and procedure of relationship strength determination was used in this research.

The instrument used to measure friendship in this study (Appendix D) and the resulting affiliation-by-affiliation asymmetric data (Appendix E), require subjects to name one another as friends. If two people name each other as friends, this satisfies the requirement of inter-rater reliability (Creswell, 2002). "In inter-rater reliability, two of more individuals observe an individual's behavior and record scores, and then the scores of the observers are compared to determine whether they are similar. This method has the advantage of obtaining observational scores from two or more individuals, thus negating any bias that might be brought on by one of the individuals" (Creswell, 2002, p.182). A network study regarding CEOs' use of friendship networks for making strategic decisions employing a similar friendship list methodology found that inter-rater agreement of reciprocal friendships to be 94% (McDonald & Westphal, 2003). In this research, only when two individual named each other as a friend was that dyad considered a strong-tie relationship. Therefore, the reciprocity of scores provided for inter-rater reliability. Other studies have also concluded validity of mutual agreement of friendship. McEvily and Zaheer (1999) tested tie bridging through similar procedures. To validate their approach, once ego-centric data regarding an individual's network were determined, they sampled the contacts the individuals named as friends and surveyed if the friendship designation was reciprocal. They found no less than 72% accuracy in friendship relationship. "Based on this analysis, it is reasonable to conclude that the validity of the ego-centric network measure is acceptable" (1999, p. 1147). Therefore, the method in this study using affiliation-by-affiliation asymmetric achieves higher levels of validity.

The criterion variable in this study was the referral results yielded from the networking activity. The BNI organization uses referral slips (Form N. 0307) to track and report on referral activity among members. These referral slips are collected, used to produce internal reports, and saved by the group's vice president. The researcher collected and accounted for each exchanged referral slip among the all relationship dyads. This manual procedure provided for reliability of referral exchange counts. The next section outlines the data collection procedure used in this study.

Data Collection

Data for this research was collected using a consistent procedure for each group and subject within the sample, following a three-step process. Step 1 was obtaining permission from each group's president to survey their members; Step 2 was attending each group's meeting and administering the survey questionnaire; and Step 3 was collecting the responses.

Step 1 of obtaining permission from each BNI group's president was important to ensure consistency regarding procedure. Each group's president was briefed prior to the procedure. It was important that the presidents incorporated time needed to administer the survey within their meeting agenda. BNI follows a close agenda for each meeting. Therefore, providing each president with knowledge about time requirements allowed the BNI meeting to proceed with little disruption. The survey procedure took place at the beginning of the meeting and took approximately ten minutes to complete. The researcher attended each group's meeting in advance to present the presidents with proper consent and receive permission. The researcher was subsequently placed on the agenda for each meeting. All groups were surveyed during the month of September 2007.

Step 2 was for the researcher to attend each meeting, distribute and review informed consent, administer the survey instrument, and answer participants' questions. The research packet included informed consent forms (Appendix A) and the survey questionnaire (Appendix D). This packet was contained in an 8" by 11" manila envelope and placed in front of each seat in the meeting space. At the beginning of the meeting, the president introduced the researcher without mention of any procedure within this research. The researcher then read the subject consent form (Appendix A) to explain the research purpose, subject involvement, voluntary participation, confidentiality, risk and benefits. It was made clear that the subjects' returning the questionnaire to the researcher represented indication that they consented to participate in this study.

Subject participation in this study was voluntary. If they chose not to participate or wished to withdraw from the study at any time, they could do so without penalty of loss of benefits. The results of the research may be published but all names associated with the data collection were held by the researcher and considered confidential. There is no foreseeable risk for participating because all data was coded to protect anonymity during the data analysis stage of the research. Once questionnaires were collected, they were immediately placed in a white folder so no other participant would have an opportunity to examine results. Although there may be no direct benefit to subjects participating, the possible benefit is to improve the understanding of networking relationships in yielding productive results for networking activities. Before subjects begin the questionnaire, they were asked if they had any questions. Once questions were answered, participants were asked to complete the instrument, which took approximately five minutes. The research procedures of presenting the study and subjects taking the instrument took approximately ten minutes.

Step 3 of the procedure was to collect all questionnaires from the participants, place them in a white envelope for transportation, and remind participants to contact the researcher if there were any further questions or concerns.

This three-step procedure was designed logically to prepare the individual group presidents for administrative coordination, proper consent and approval, and to eliminate any research bias. The instrument was administered at the beginning of each meeting, prior to any exchange of referrals, which could influence a subject's response because of immediate consideration during that meeting. If a subject received a favorable referral during the meeting, there could be a bias of response based on emotional reward at that time. Therefore, placing the procedure at the beginning of the meeting eliminated this potential bias. Collecting the instrument upon the subject's completion and placing it in a different colored envelope reduces any perceived risk of subject bias of response. If subjects understood that a member they did not name as a friend would not see the results they are more likely to respond accurately within the instrument. The next section discusses data analysis plan and techniques.

Data Analysis

The research survey instrument and the referral sharing data maintained by the BNI groups provided the data necessary for determining a correlation among variables. The survey instrument (Appendix D) measured relationship tie-strength and some possible intervening variables. The criterion variable of referral results was determined through content analysis of data maintained by each BNI group. This data was coded and arranged in an affiliation-by-affiliation asymmetric data matrix (Appendix E) to determine tie-strength relationships that existed within the sample. This study's hypotheses were based on a relationship between network dyads within 10 individual BNI groups. Several groups were tested for the purposes of achieving a statistically significant sample size for this study. However, these groups shared the context of goal-directedness and are considered to be one larger group within the study population.

For the predictor variable of tie-strength, four ordinal measures were identified: (1) no relationship, (2), acquaintance, (3) friend, and (4) close friend. Ordinal measures "...provide response options where participants rank from best or most important to worst or least important some trait or attribute, or characteristic" (Creswell, 2002, p. 172). For the criterion variable in this study, the amount of referrals traded among dyads is integer data.

Nonparametric statistics analyzes data that contain no assumption about population parameters or distribution (Sheskin, 2004). This study made no assumption regarding population distribution. However, the nature of the data collected suggested that the distribution of the population may be non-normal (Sheskin, 2004).

Creswell (2002) emphasizes the number of variables required for a correlation approach. This study's focus was on one predictor variable (relationship-tie strength) and one criterion variable (referral results). Variable measurements that the data represents determine the type of statistical test used. This study's data represented ordinal measures for the predictor variable and integer measures for the criterion variable. The statistical test used in this study to satisfy the research question and hypotheses was the Kruskal-Wallis one-way analysis of variance by rank, a nonparametric test used when data is ordinal (Sheskin, 2004).

The only deviation from statistical theory regarding the use of the Kruskal-Wallis test is that this study's criterion variable is not continuous. Referral data represented integer data. According to Sheskin (2004), this deviation is common because dependent variable results are often discreetly random, and researchers have no control over the distribution of the continuous data reported. A t-test for independent samples is not appropriate because outliers have an effect on variability, subsequently affecting the impact on the sample means. The Kruskal-Wallis test reduces the impact of outliers by ranking the data. The Kruskal-Wallis one-way analysis of variance by rank was applied to all variable groups (tie-strength), and refined further to determine the statistical significance between strong- and weak-tie groups.

The predictor variable results (tie strength) were transposed from the survey instruments the subjects completed to Microsoft Excel spreadsheets. These spreadsheets produced affiliation-by-affiliation asymmetric data matrixes (Appendix E) for each group, and then were consolidated for data analysis. The statistical software tool used for this study's data and statistical analysis was JMP 7, which provides many statistical applications for business, engineering and educational use (www.jmp.com, n.d.). In this study, JMP 7 calculated statistical analysis for Kruskal-Wallis, logistical regression, goodness-of-fit, and logistical fit of various combinations of data. A research assistant used JMP 7 software to produce this study's results.

Validity and Reliability

A research study's design can be compromised by statistical, construct, internal and external validity risk (Creswell, 2002). "A threat to validity means statistical and design issues may threaten the experiment so that the conclusions reached from the data may provide false readings about possible causation – the relationship between the treatment and the outcome" (p. 324). This research has minimized these risks.

Statistical validity is achieved through the utilization of standard network research procedures. By combining Bowler and Brass' (2006) scoring approach with Kilduff's (1992) matrix approach, a clear dyad relationship matrix was constructed. The resulting tie-strength dyads established served the purposes of this study's predictor variable data for correlation to the criterion variable of referral results. The criterion variable of referral results was derived through content analysis of records kept by each BNI group. These approaches are well established in the literature and considered valid and appropriate for this study. In addition, the heterogeneous sample of all group members within each BNI group was achieved, and the environmental factors were controlled through the BNI forum. No statistical threat to validity was expected.

Construct validity was achieved by providing good and clear definitions of variables (Creswell, 2002). Friendship is a primary measure of relationship and is considered the best single measure of tie-strength (Jenssen & Koenig, 2002). Within the literature, tie-strength is considered an outcome of closeness based on emotional intensity within a relationship (Burt, 1992; Granovetter, 1973; Ibarra, 1997). Construct validity threat was also reduced through multiple measures. Within this study procedure, subjects must achieve a mutual perspective of friendship with one another for the relationship to be considered strong. Any apprehensiveness of subjects was controlled through the research procedure of obtaining consent and maintaining confidentiality. No construct validity issues for this study were anticipated.

Internal validity for this study was maintained through carefully constructed experimental procedures. "Threats to internal validity are problems that threaten drawing correct inferences that arise because of experimental procedures or the experience of participants" (Creswell, 2002, p. 325). Possible threats to this study's internal validity were history, maturation, regression, selection, mortality, interactions with selection, and diffusion of treatment factors. History validity threats regard "Time passing between the beginning of the experiment and the end" (p. 325). Maturation threats regard "individuals developing or changing during the experiment" (p. 325). Both history and maturation are controlled through the briefness of the experimental procedure. It was expected that the instrument would successfully be applied to a group of 30 individuals in 10 minutes at the beginning of their membership meeting. Regression and selection threats to the procedure depend on the sample selection bias (Creswell, 2002). Since all participants were included for each group there was no validity risk. There were only two possible validity threats: mortality and diffusion of treatment.

Mortality validity risk is when participants drop out (Creswell, 2002). Because of the procedure used, obtaining leadership permission, conducting the experiment in 10 minutes, and the absence of foreseeable individual risk, it was expected that most members of each group would participate.

Diffusion of treatment validity risk is "When the experimental and control groups can communicate with each other" (Creswell, 2002, p. 326). While there is no control group in this study, subjects in varying groups could communicate with one another outside the group meetings. Therefore, this research procedure included conducting all experiments with all ten groups within a four-week time frame.

External validity in research is the ability to claim generalizability regarding the sample data to other situations, setting or people (Creswell, 2002). Creswell (2002) emphasizes three external validity risks: interaction of selection, setting, and history and their treatments. Interaction of selection and treatment risk is when generalization about the population studied is not representative of the total population. This risk was minimized in this study by allowing all members within the groups the right to participate. In addition, participation was made easy for all involved through expedient procedures.

Interaction of setting and treatment validity risk exists when generalizations cannot be made across other settings (Creswell, 2002). Since all research subjects are BNI members who follow strict procedural meeting protocol, generalizations can be made regarding this study's results across BNI groups outside the sample.

Interaction of history and treatment validity risk exists when generalizations cannot be made about past or future findings (Creswell, 2002). "One solution is to replicate the study at a later time rather than try to generalize results to other times" (p. 328). This study does not attempt to generalize about the past or future. Rather, this study represents the networking relationships that exist during a three-month period. Future research can replicate this study to reduce this risk.

Based on close adherence to standard network research tools, procedures, design, and parallels to other tie-strength research, this study was appropriate to answer the research question. The next section provides a summary of this chapter.

Summary

The purpose of this quantitative predictive correlational research study was to examine the economic value of relationship-tie development within a contemporary goal-directed networking organization. To fulfill this purpose, members of a goal-directed business development networking group, BNI, in New Hampshire were surveyed to determine relationship strength among the members. The predictor variable (tie-strength) was measured through network adjacency matrix analysis to determine weak-tie and strong-tie relationship dyads (Kilduff & Tsai, 2006). This matrix methodology is applied prolifically in network research because it establishes reciprocal friendship relationships among members of a network (Scott, 2003). Once dyad strength was determined, content analyses of membership referral records were measured for correlation. Intervening variables were also measured, including frequency of member one-on-one meetings outside the group's formal meeting, frequency of membership meeting attendance, frequency of attendance at group training provided by the organization, and time within a dyad's profession.

This study was unique because it measured results for relationship strength in a context and construct designed to elicit referral results for weak relationship development. Therefore, if strong relationship correlates to results, or improves results for reciprocating relationship actors, a case may be made for the value of strong-tie relationships for the purposes of dyad productive economic value in the context of contemporary networking groups.

The procedure used in this study was appropriate, followed a logical progression, and can be easily replicated within other goal-directed organizations. Minimal control was necessary beyond application of the instrument because control is embedded in the sample organization policies, rules, and procedures. The population sampled was small and micro-business people who are members of the New Hampshire BNI organization, generally defined as entrepreneurs, innovators and smaller enterprises consisting of business owners or small businesses representatives. Of the 10 BNI groups in the total group target sample of 239 members, 184 responses were collected. It was estimated that a minimum of 50 (n=50) strong-tie dyad relationships would result from analysis of all groups measured.

The statistical test used in this study to satisfy the research question and hypotheses was the Kruskal-Wallis one-way analysis of variance by rank, a nonparametric test used when data is ordinal (Sheskin, 2004). While no deviation from the Kruskal-Wallis test was anticipated, unforeseen results required the researcher to refine the statistical results using logistical regression. Logistical regression is a multivariate statistic used to produce linear combinations of predictor variables (Sheskin, 2004). The Kruskal-Wallis one-way analysis of variance by rank (non-parametric statistic) fulfilled the purpose of this research.

Chapter 4 reports the data findings of all variables and relevant statistical analysis for correlation. In addition, data collection variances, and any deviation from this study's proposed procedures are disclosed. This chapter will begin with a summary the study's purpose, and research question, and transition the reader to possible larger meaning of results to be presented in Chapter 5.

CHAPTER 4: DATA ANALYSIS

The purpose of this quantitative predictive correlational research study was to examine the economic value of relationship-tie development within a contemporary goal-directed networking organization. To fulfill this purpose, members of a goal-directed business development networking group, Business Network International (BNI) in New Hampshire, were surveyed to determine relationship strength among the members. The predictor variable (tie-strength) was measured through network adjacency matrix analysis to determine weak-tie and strong-tie relationship dyads (Kilduff & Tsai, 2006). Once dyad strength was determined, a content analysis of membership referral records was measured for correlation. This chapter illustrates and explains the procedure and results of data development and application of statistical tests for analysis.

Chapter 3 described this research study's methodology, design and appropriateness, examined how variables were objectified, and justified the research question and hypothesis. In addition, the subject sample frame, research procedures, instrument development, data collection, data analysis, validity and reliability were outlined. Chapter 4 describes the results of network adjacency matrix analysis (tie-strength), content analysis (referrals traded) and the statistical methods applied to these variables. The Kruskal-Wallis one-way analysis of variance by rank was applied to the variables to determine statistical significance between the variable results. Additionally, logistical regression of the variables was applied for more refined analysis. This chapter presents a review of the research procedure, methodology, and describes the results in the context the research question and hypothesis that underline this study. Furthermore, conclusions are drawn regarding the statistical significant of relationship strength in predicting referral results for network actors.

Research Design and Methodology

This study examined the dyad relationships and referral trading results for the membership of 10 BNI groups in the greater Manchester New Hampshire area. To determine dyad relationship strength (predictor variable), network adjacency matrix analysis was used. This method is a relational data-sorting procedure used in social network analysis (Scott, 2003). The results of this method compared mutual relationships that were linked and the associated strength of those relationships. Referral trading among the dyads (criterion variable) was determined through a content analysis of documented referral results collected by each group.

Data was successfully collected from 10 of the 12 targeted BNI groups during the month of September 2007. One group withdrew from the study 2 weeks prior to data collection and one group disbanded the week of data collection. The 10 groups that did participate in this study had a total target sample population of 239 members, of which 184 (n=184) participated and completed the survey. Therefore, the sample response rate was 77% from the total sample populations. Of the surveys collected, only four were removed from the study's results because they were not complete. Because this study used network adjacency matrix analysis to determine dyad relationships, all the relationship data collected for the members who were not present at the time of survey, or did not complete the survey, were removed. The data that remains in the analysis is only for intact identified dyad relationships. Content data for the referrals of all participants traded for the three-month sample frame (June through August 2007) was collected from each group's vice-president at the time the survey was administered.

Sampling Method and Procedure

Data for this research was collected using a consistent procedure for each group and subject within the sample, following a three-step process. Step 1 was planning with each group's vice-president to survey the members; Step 2 was attending each group's meeting and administering the survey questionnaire; and Step 3 was collecting the responses.

To ensure consistency regarding use of the subjects, each group's vice-president was briefed in June 2007, prior to the procedure. Providing each vice-president with knowledge about time requirements allowed the BNI meeting to proceed with little disruption. The survey procedure took place at the beginning of the meeting and in all cases took less than ten minutes to complete. All groups were surveyed in September 2007.

The researcher attended each group meeting, distributed and reviewed informed consent, administered the survey instrument, and answered participants' questions. At the beginning of each meeting, each group's president introduced the researcher without mention of any procedure within the research. The researcher distributed the informed consent form (Appendix A) attached to the survey questionnaire (Appendix D). The researcher then read the subject consent form (Appendix A) that explained the research purpose, subject involvement, voluntary participation, confidentiality, risk and benefits. This distribution procedure concluded with a statement that the subjects' returning the questionnaire to the researcher was indication that they consented to participate in this study. Once questionnaires were completed, they were collected and immediately placed in a white folder so no other participant had an opportunity to examine results. The researcher thanked the group for their time, collected the referral results slips from the vice-president, and exited the meeting. This procedure was repeated with each group during the month of September 2007 until all 10 groups were complete.

Development of the Intervention, Surveys, and Questionnaire

For the purposes of measuring the predictor variable of tie-strength, affiliation-by-affiliation asymmetric data analysis was used in this study (Scott, 2003). This matrix methodology is applied prolifically in network research because it establishes reciprocal friendship relationships among members of a network. As depicted in Appendix E, relationship data are presented in a rectangular matrix and indicate the reciprocal friendship relations through egocentric measurement. To establish the necessary friendship relationships that exist within a network, a survey was produced using a well accepted methodology in network research (Bowler & Brass, 2006; Kilduff, 1992). By combining Bowler and Brass' (2006) scoring approach with Kilduff's (1992) matrix approach, a clear dyad relationship matrix was constructed. Each of the 10 BNI group studied received a list of its members and was asked to report the strength of their relationships with each other. Appendix D represents the questionnaire developed for this purpose.

An additional data inquiry was added at the end of each survey for the subjects to answer. These questions provide insight into the maturity of the sample's network activity and indicate use of prescribed BNI principles and group goal-directed activity.

Data Preparation

This section describes and presents the method of data organization and consolidation. This study uses network adjacency matrix analysis to develop affiliation-by-affiliation asymmetric data (Scott, 2003). This method requires survey data to be coded and organized for dyad and tie-strength comparison. Furthermore, once data was organized appropriately, referral trading results were matched with each dyad and further sorted for statistical application. The final dataset of dyad and referral results for all 10 groups sampled were combined and tested for statistical significance.

Within the network literature, there is no standard definition of tie-strength (Jack, 2005). Variations among research studies are minimal and only vary based on categorical definition of friendship. In a study of job attainment, researchers used friends and acquaintances to separate strong from weak-ties (Granovetter, 1983). In a study of business start-ups, the degree of friendship was measured based on close friend, friend, and acquaintance definitions (Jenssen & Koenig, 2002). A study of tie-strength activation for an entrepreneur defined relationship strength based on friends, friends of friends, family, and other characterizations (Jack, 2005). This study utilized Bowler and Brass' (2006) definitions and procedures for determining tie-strength and categorizes relationships based on matching of relationship strength among participants. Each participant identified group peers as either (1) no relationship, (2) acquaintance, (3) friend, or (4) close friend. By matching each possible dyad and its identified relationship affiliation-by-affiliation, a network adjacency matrix was produced. Appendix E represents an example of result of that analysis for one of the 10 groups sampled.

A network adjacency matrix is a relational data-sorting instrument used in social network analysis (Scott, 2003). It represents a direct comparison of mutual relations that are linked, and shows the actual ties among the network actors. This tie relationship information was collected and documented in an asymmetrical adjacency matrix. Asymmetrical refers to the lack of symmetry in relations among the network actors (Kilduff & Tsai, 2006). Therefore, if one actor chooses another as a friend, and the other does not reciprocate that relationship, the data contained within a network matrix is considered asymmetrical. Symmetry indicates a strong-tie among actors, and asymmetry indicates a weak-tie relationship. This study's predictor variable is tie-strength, which is identified by the symmetry or asymmetry of the data within the (Appendix E) adjacency matrix tables.

Surveys collected by group were organized and consolidated into 10 adjacent matrix tables (one for each group sampled). The relationship table organized each member's relationship with one another. The survey questionnaire and matrix tables were ordered alphabetically by type of business so that data could be easily transitioned from survey to tables. Once all relationship data was populated on the relationship table, relationship strength was determined by comparing data symmetry.

Determining tie-strength relies on the concept of mutual choice (Granovetter, 1973). Regardless of a tie-definition, if two people (a dyad) mutually choose one another as holding a certain relationship, a tie of some dimension exists. If two people are asked to list their friends, and both choose each other, it is concluded they are friends. Figure 9 illustrates the 10 possible dyad relationship combinations based on the 4 relationship choices used in this study.

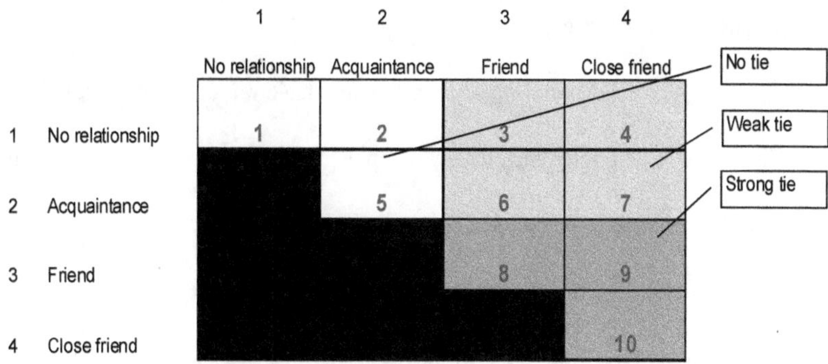

Figure 9. Tie relationship dyad combinations.

Based on the method of mutuality, this study combined the 10 possible combinations into three relationship categories: no-tie, weak-tie and strong-tie relationships. If two people in a dyad reported mutual friendship, the relationship was considered strong. If only one person in a dyad reported some level of friendship, the relationship was considered weak. A relationship exists to some extent if one member feels some level of emotional intensity. Since that emotional intensity is not mutual, the relationship is not considered strong. Dyads reporting no relationship and acquaintance relationship are considered to possess no friendship relationship. They know each other, but the relationship lacks emotional intensity necessary for a friendship (Ibarra, 1997; Granovetter, 1973, Burt, 1992).

Once adjacency matrix tables were populated with survey results, dyad relationships were color coded into the three tie-strength categories. Each table was then mathematically tied-out horizontally and vertically to ensure that the visual count analysis was accurate.

Once the relationship adjacency matrix table was complete for relationship information, referral trading data was populated into adjacent matrix tables. An example of these tables is represented in Appendix F. This was accomplished through a content analysis of the referral slips collected from each group at the time of application of the survey procedure. This was done manually by reviewing each referral slip traded within each group. All referral slips that contained member dyad names were recorded within the referral trading adjacency matrix. All referrals that did not include a participating member dyad were removed from the data.

From the relationship and referral trading adjacent matrixes for all 10 groups sampled, a dataset of the entire sample was compiled using Microsoft Excel. This procedure included transforming the adjacent matrixes for each group into one spreadsheet depicting each individual's relationship with group peers (relationship of referrer to referee), the resulting relationship strength of that dyad relationship (strong, weak, or no relationship) and the number of referrals traded (from referrer to referee). This dataset was further sorted by relationship strength yielding data necessary to apply the Kruskal-Wallis one-way analysis of a variance and regression of ordinal data. Figure 10 highlights the relationship results and referral counts for each group and the results from the total sample.

Group name	Member size	Member sample	Relationship strength (Diad)						Referrals traded					
			Strong-Tie: Symmetric Friendship (F/F, F/CF, CF/CF)	Relation distribution %	Weak-Tie: Asymmetric Friendship (NT/F, NR/CF, A/F, A,CF)	Relation distribution %	No-Tie: No Friendship	Relation distribution %	Strong-Tie	%	Weak-Tie	%	No-Tie	%
Group 1	42	34	80	14%	117	14%	364	65%	42	53%	74	63%	77	21%
Group 2	32	29	84	21%	99	19%	223	55%	48	57%	33	33%	29	13%
Group 3	25	16	16	13%	34	22%	70	58%	10	63%	21	62%	20	29%
Group 4	24	15	26	25%	38	35%	41	39%	8	31%	10	26%	9	22%
Group 5	24	17	26	19%	51	35%	59	45%	16	62%	19	37%	11	19%
Group 6	24	20	38	20%	51	21%	101	63%	57	150%	41	80%	56	65%
Group 7	20	15	25	24%	36	32%	44	42%	21	84%	35	07%	33	75%
Group 8	18	14	12	13%	31	28%	48	53%	3	25%	13	42%	13	27%
Group 9	15	12	9	14%	32	54%	25	38%	22	244%	51	159%	22	83%
Group 10	15	12	7	11%	24	31%	35	53%	4	57%	8	33%	16	46%
Sum	239	184	323	17%	513	22%	1010	55%	231	72%	305	53%	286	26%

Figure 10. Summary of dataset results of relationship strength and referral trading.

The next section describes the results from the demographic questions included in this research study.

Demographic Data

During the survey procedure, demographic information was collected to add insight into the BNI context maturity of the sample population. This included length of affiliation in the goal-directed group, frequency of meetings with members outside the group, frequency of attendance of training events hosted by the goal-directed organization, and time in profession. Appendix D represents the demographic questions asked. This information adds context about the sample participants and validates the level of understanding and practice in a networking setting. Of the total sample (n=184), data for 175 members were retained for analysis. The 9 responses left out of the analysis were due to responses being skipped or not fully completed. A summary of responses to these demographic questions is presented in Appendix G. The following paragraphs explain these results.

Data regarding length of participation in a BNI group was collected for the sample. The results determined that 84% of the respondents (n=175) had been members of BNI for more than 6 months. Therefore, most respondents had familiarity with the BNI networking context and practices.

The BNI network context of referral sharing is supported by peer meetings outside the scheduled BNI meetings. This practice facilitates relationship building and knowing BNI peer referral requirements and preferences. BNI calls this practice of meeting outside the regularly schedule meetings *one-on-one* meetings. When asked the number of one-on-one meetings the respondents (n=175) participated in, 48% reported they participated in one or two meetings outside the group per month and 42% reported they participated in more than 3 additional meeting per month. The limitation to this response is that participants had no place in the questionnaire to report zero meetings. However, no member called attention to this optional undocumented choice. It is possible that many of those who reported having between one and two meetings per month gave inappropriate responses. Therefore it is concluded that more than 42% participate in relationship building outside regular schedule BNI meetings.

Attending BNI training is required of new members in the first six months of their membership. However, after initial training is complete, the BNI organization only recommends additional training, and provides various training sessions monthly. When asked the number of training events or seminars members had attended in the previous 12 months, 78% of the participants (n=175) reported they attended at least one training meeting in the previous year. Only 23% reported that they attended more than three training meetings per year, and 22% reported they attended no additional training event each year. This suggests that most BNI members who participated in this study continue to learn and reinforce their BNI practice methods at least once per year outside BNI regular meetings.

Profession (vocation) and employment demographic information was collected. Respondents reported (n=175) in the BNI sample that 53% were in their profession for more than 4 years. Only 21% reported they were new to their profession (less than one year). Therefore, most participants have been practicing their profession for more than one year. A limitation to this question is there was no place to answer between three and four years in their profession. No respondent varied from the provided responses.

When asked how long they were affiliated with their current company (firm), 31% of participants (n=175) reported less than one year, and 69% reported more than one year. A limitation to this question is that there was no place to answer between three and four years with their current firm. No respondent varied from the provided responses.

One demographic question asked participants (n=175) to describe their affiliation with their firm. Sixteen percent reported they were self-employed owners of a firm with no employees, and 43% reported they owned a small business with less than 10 employees. Therefore, 59% of the sample represented owners of a small business, and 41% reported that they were employed by a firm. Fifteen percent of these were of a firm with less than 10 employees and 26% of a firm with more than 10 employees. This suggests that the BNI sample represented 74% of businesses with less than 10 employees. A limitation of this question is there was no place for participants to respond that they owned a firm with more than 10 employees.

The length of affiliation in the goal-directed group, frequency of meetings with members outside the group, frequency of attendance of training events hosted by the goal-directed organization, and time in profession provided some insight into the perspective of the networking actors. These limited data results provide a superficial context to the sample participants' demographic position in their professional community. However, these results validate that most BNI participants in the sample group have a level of experience with the practices of networking in the BNI goal-directed context.

Statistical Method

Nonparametric statistics analyzes data that contain no assumption about population parameters or distribution (Sheskin, 2004). This study made no assumption regarding population distribution. However, a single sample test for evaluating population skewness or goodness-of-fit (Appendix H) indicates that the distribution of the population is non-normal (Sheskin, 2004). Variable measurements that the data represents also determine the type of statistical test used. This study's data represent ordinal measures for the predictor variable and integer measures for the criterion variable. The statistical test used in this study to satisfy the research question and hypotheses is the Kruskal-Wallis one-way analysis of variance by rank, a nonparametric test used when data is ordinal (Sheskin, 2004).

The only deviation from statistical theory regarding the use of the Kruskal-Wallis test is that this study's criterion variable is not continuous. Referral data represents integer data. According to Sheskin (2004), this deviation is common because dependent variable results are often discreetly random, and researchers have no control over the distribution of the continuous data reported. A t-test for independent samples is not appropriate because outliers have an effect on variability, subsequently affecting the impact on the sample means. The Kruskal-Wallis test reduces the impact of outliers by ranking the data. The Kruskal-Wallis one-way analysis of variance by rank was applied to all variable groups (tie-strength), and refined further to determine the statistical significance between strong- and weak-tie groups.

This study also employed logistical regression to refine the results obtained by the Kruskal-Wallis one-way analysis of the variance by rank. Logistical regression is a multivariate statistic used to produce linear combinations of predictor variables (Sheskin, 2004). Because the Kruskal-Wallis test produced unforeseen results it was necessary to further analyze tie-strength dyad relationships' effect on the criterion variable. Specifically, the logistical regression allowed for a statistical explanation for failing to reject the null hypotheses.

The software tools used for this study's data and statistical analysis were JMP 7 and Microsoft Excel. JMP 7 provides many statistical applications for business, engineering and educational use (www.jmp.com, n.d.). In this study, JMP 7 calculated statistical analysis for Kruskal-Wallis, logistical regression, goodness-of-fit, and logistical fit of various combinations of data. Microsoft Excel was used for all data recording, sorting and analysis. A research assistant used these software tools to produce this study's results. The hypotheses and each analysis process and results are reported in the sections that follow.

Research Question and Hypotheses

The present research considered the impact of relationship strength in the context and construct of goal-directed networking groups. The following research question is reflective of this study's framework and purpose: Is there an association between relationship tie-strength and goal-directed outcomes for members of structured

networking goal-directed organizations? To answer this research question, this study

sought to support a null or alternative hypothesis. "Null hypothesis make a prediction that

in the general population there is no relationship between variables or no difference

between groups on measured variables....In a directional hypothesis, the researcher

predicts the direction of relationship for measured variables in a population" (Creswell,

2002, p. 143). The fundamental alternative hypothesis established in this study was that

relationship strength and referral trading output possess a positive relationship that is

statistically significant. Moreover, the nature of a dyad relationship, being strong, weak,

or nonexistent, would have an effect on the referral results people experience.

Using the Kruskal-Wallis one-way analysis of variance by rank statistical test, the

mean of the rank for population groups were measured and compared (Sheskin, 2004).

The null hypothesis in this study is that there is no relationship ($p>.05$) between tie-

strength and referral outcome of the population sampled. For the null to be rejected for

significance, the chi-square value must be equal or greater than $p>.05$. The alternative

hypotheses is that there is a relationship ($p<.05$) between tie-strength and referral

outcome for members of a goal-directed networking group population sample. The

following section provides the statistical analysis of the dataset results.

Presentation of Results

Relationship tie-strength data from 184 individuals (n=184) was collected from

10 Business Networking International (BNI) groups in the greater Manchester New

Hampshire area. This data produced relationship dyad counts for strong, weak and no tie

relationship groups. As a result, 3,692 one-way relationship measures to other group members were collected, and 1,846 dyad relationships were accounted for in this research. Referrals traded among the dyads were collected and accounted for to compare and correlate to dyad economic value. In this study, 822 referrals were traded among the members and accounted for.

This section reports the results of statistical methods applied to this study's variables. The Kruskal-Wallis one-way analysis of variance by rank was applied to the variables to determine statistical significant between the variable results. Logistic regression of the variables was also applied for more refined analysis. The results are presented in the following logical order: (a) Kruskal-Wallis comparison of all group data for one-way individual relationship perspectives and tie-strength (strong, weak and no relationship), (b) comparison of tie-strength group by group for one-way relationship perspectives and dyad tie strength relationship (no relationship compared to weak relationship; no relationship to strong relationship; strong relationship to weak relationship), and (c) logistical regression of ordinal data for all groups. Results and conclusions are presented for all data and statistical analysis. All results were calculated using JMP 7 software.

Variable Results for All Data

Data from 184 participants (n=184) within 10 separate BNI groups was received that defined their relationship to their group member peers. This represented a response rate of 77% from the sample population. Referrals traded among these group members were matched to each member for a total count of 822 referrals traded. Table 5 presents the results of the one-way perspective of relationship. This data accounts for every score and referral provided to a peer from only one participant's perspective, with a total of 3,692 possible one-way relationship perspectives.

Table 5. *One-way relationship scores and counts for all participants*

	One way relationship score & counts for all participants				
	1	2	3	4	
	No relationship	Acquaintance	Friend	Close friend	Total
One way relationship score	403	2130	986	173	3692
Referral count	31	391	292	108	822
% ref traded / relationship score	8%	18%	30%	62%	22%

The percentage of referrals traded using this one-way perspective suggests that a member is more likely to give a higher percentage of referrals based on a one-way friendship strength perspective. Therefore, those who are considered a close friend to another receive a higher percentage of referrals. Using the Kruskal-Wallis one-way analysis of the variance validates that this difference is significant (Chi Square <.0001) as depicted in Figure 11. This indicates that the difference in the mean scores between at least two sample groups is significant (Sheskin, 2004).

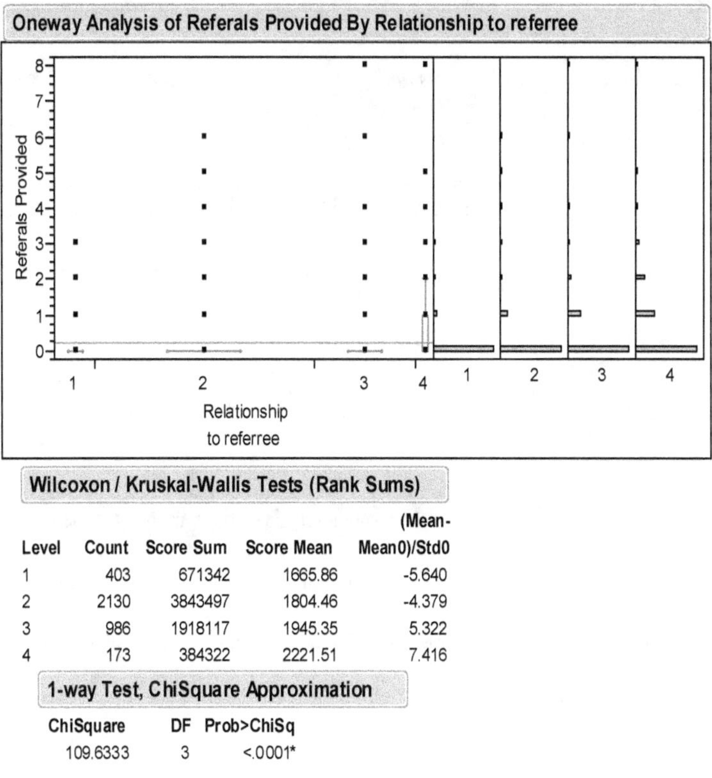

Wilcoxon / Kruskal-Wallis Tests (Rank Sums)

Level	Count	Score Sum	Score Mean	(Mean-Mean0)/Std0
1	403	671342	1665.86	-5.640
2	2130	3843497	1804.46	-4.379
3	986	1918117	1945.35	5.322
4	173	384322	2221.51	7.416

1-way Test, ChiSquare Approximation

ChiSquare	DF	Prob>ChiSq
109.6333	3	<.0001*

Figure 11. One-way analysis of referrals provided by relationship to referee.

When data was matched and grouped into dyads for comparison, strong-tie

relationships also appeared to receive more referrals than those dyad relationships that

were weaker. Table 6 presents the breakout of relationships into dyads and the referrals

trade among these groups.

Table 6. *Dyad relationship scores and counts for all participants.*

Dyad relationship score & counts for all participants			
1-1, 1-2, 2-2	1-3. 2-3, 4-1, 4-2	3-3, 3-4, 4-4	
Strong-tie	**Weak-tie**	**No-tie**	**Total**
323	513	1010	1846
231	305	286	822
72%	59%	28%	45%

(row labels: Dyad relationship score; Referral count; % ref traded / dyad)

Using the Kruskal-Wallis one-way analysis of the variance test demonstrates that there is also significance among these differences. This indicates that the difference in the mean between at least two sample groups is significant (Sheskin, 2004). Figure 12 presents this finding.

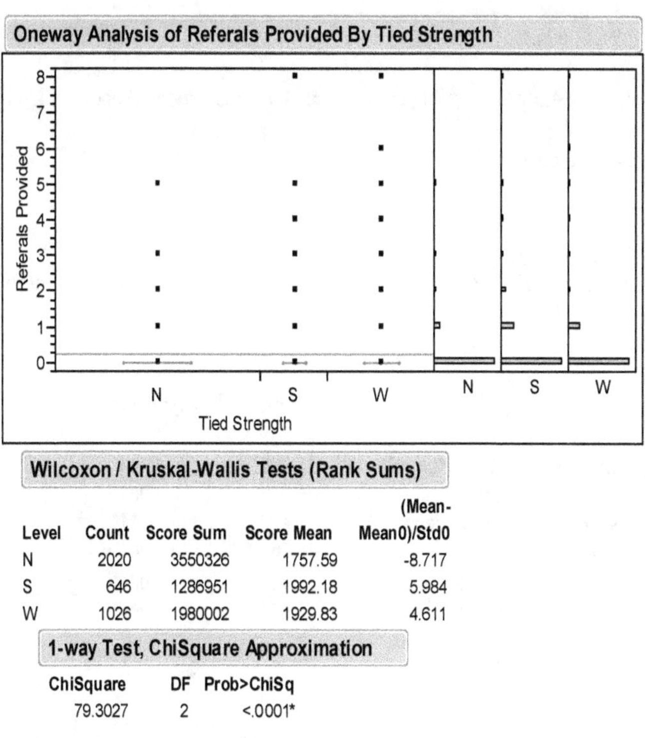

Wilcoxon / Kruskal-Wallis Tests (Rank Sums)

Level	Count	Score Sum	Score Mean	(Mean-Mean0)/Std0
N	2020	3550326	1757.59	-8.717
S	646	1286951	1992.18	5.984
W	1026	1980002	1929.83	4.611

1-way Test, ChiSquare Approximation

ChiSquare	DF	Prob>ChiSq
79.3027	2	<.0001*

Figure 12. One-way analysis of referrals provided by dyad tie strength.

Therefore, based on the analyses of all dyad groups, the data suggests that there are

significant differences among at least two possible dyad and one-way relationship

perspectives (Sheskin, 2004).

Variable Results for Group by Group Data

To refine the understanding of significance among all groups the Kruskal-Wallis

test was applied to all possible combinations of groups (one degree of freedom). When

comparing ordinal data for nonparametric statistical tests with only two independent

samples (k=2) the Mann-Whitney U test is appropriate (Sheskin, 2004). However, the

Kruskal-Wallis one-way analysis of variance will provide an equivalent result. Therefore a one-way relationship perspective from referrer to referee was completed using the

Kruskal-Wallis test for all possible combinations as presented in Appendix I. Table 7

summarizes these results.

Table 7. *Kruskal-Wallis test for one-way analysis of referrals provided by relationship to referee.*

			Chi square	Significance
No relationship	/	Acquaintance	17.265	<.0001*
No relationship	/	Friend	46.063	<.0001*
No relationship	/	Close friend	81.452	<.0001*
Acquaintance	/	Friend	28.763	<.0001*
Acquaintance	/	Close friend	61.434	<.0001*
Friend	/	Close friend	19.004	<.0001*

When applying the Kruskal-Wallis test to relationship dyad combinations, the

results were less consistent than those from the one-way relationship test. Appendix I

presents the detailed analysis for these tests. Table 8 presents a summary of these results.

Table 8. *Kruskal-Wallis test for referrals provided by tie strength.*

			Chi square	Significance
No tie	/	Weak tie	48.320	<.0001*
No tie	/	Strong tie	63.836	<.0001*
Weak tie	/	Strong tie	2.754	0.0970

Specifically, when comparing weak ties to strong ties using the Kruskal-Wallis test, this

study found the result to not be significant at a < .05 level. Figure 13 presents the result

for this comparison.

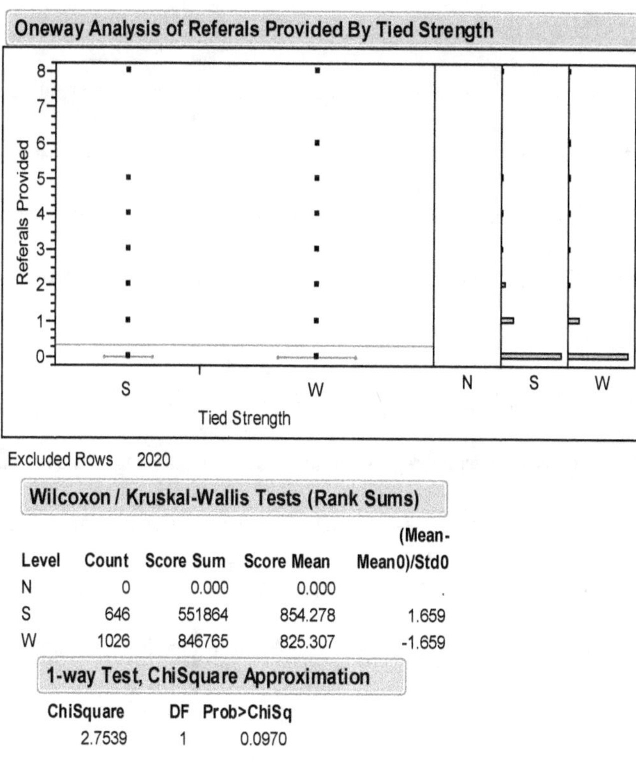

Excluded Rows   2020

Wilcoxon / Kruskal-Wallis Tests (Rank Sums)

Level	Count	Score Sum	Score Mean	(Mean-Mean0)/Std0
N	0	0.000	0.000	.
S	646	551864	854.278	1.659
W	1026	846765	825.307	-1.659

1-way Test, ChiSquare Approximation

ChiSquare	DF	Prob>ChiSq
2.7539	1	0.0970

Figure 13. One-way analysis of referrals provided between weak and strong tie strength.

These results suggest a contradiction between one-way relationship referral giving and dyad referral giving. A one-way perspective, in which one person's friendship perspective of another, results in more referrals received for the person who is perceived as a friend. Dyad relationship where there is mutual reciprocation of that friendship perspective did not result in more referrals traded to these dyad members. Therefore, this study failed to reject the null hypothesis that there is no difference between tie strength and referral outcome of members of a goal-directed networking group. However, there were statistically significant results to suggest that what one person perceives the relationship to be will result in a positive referral receiving outcome.

Because the Kruskal-Wallis tests produced contradictions in the results, it was necessary to further analyze tie-strength dyad relationships' effect on the criterion variable. Specifically, a logistical regression allowed for a statistical explanation for failing to reject the null hypotheses. The next section presents and considers these logistical regression results.

Variable Results of Dyads using Logistical Regression

This study used logistical regression to refine understanding of the results obtained by the Kruskal-Wallis one-way analysis of the variance by rank. Logistical regression is a multivariate statistic used to produce linear combinations of predictor variables (Sheskin, 2004). Because the Kruskal-Wallis test produced unforeseen results, it was necessary to further analyze tie-strength dyad relationships' effect on the criterion variable. Specifically, the logistical regression allowed for a statistical explanation for failing to reject the null hypotheses.

This study grouped tie strength into ordinal data dyad groups (strong, weak and no-tie dyad relationships) based on previous literature. Determining tie-strength relied on the concept of mutual choice (Granovetter, 1973). Regardless of a tie-definition, if two people (a dyad) mutually choose one another as holding a certain relationship, a tie of some dimension exists. If two people are asked to list their friends, and both choose each other, it is concluded they are friends. Therefore, there were 10 possible dyad relationship combinations based on the 4 relationship choices used in this study. Figure 14 presents these combinations and the resulting dyad and referral counts.

		1 No relationship	2 Acquaintance	3 Friend	4 Close friend
1	**No relationship**	**1-1**	**1-2**	**1-3**	**1-4**
	Dyad count	66	238	32	1
	Referral count	5	33	20	0
	% ref traded	8%	14%	63%	0%
2	**Acquaintance**		**2-2**	**2-3**	**2-4**
	Dyad count		706	444	36
	Referral count		248	248	37
	% ref traded		35%	56%	103%
3	**Friend**			**3-3**	**3-4**
	Dyad count			210	89
	Referral count			111	87
	% ref traded			53%	98%
4	**Close friend**				**4-4**
	Dyad count				24
	Referral count				33
	% ref traded				138%

Figure 14. Ten tie relationship dyad combinations and associated dyad and referral counts.

Based on the method of mutuality, this study combined the 10 possible combinations into 3 relationship categories: no-tie, weak-tie and strong-tie relationships. If two people in a dyad reported mutual friendship, the relationship was considered strong. If only one person in a dyad reported some level of friendship the relationship was considered weak. A relationship existed to some extent if one member felt some level of emotional intensity. If emotional intensity was not mutual, the relationship was not considered strong. No-relationship and acquaintance-relationship dyads were considered to possess no friendship relationship. They knew each other, but the relationship lacked emotional intensity necessary for a friendship (Ibarra, 1997; Granovetter, 1973, Burt, 1992).

Using the established definition of dyad strength groupings produced evidence to reject the null hypothesis that there is no difference (P>.05) between tie-strength and referral outcome of members of a goal-directed networking group. When analyzing all 10 groups separately, anomalies in the dyad data emerge. Figure 15 demonstrates that the percentages of referrals within the 10 possible dyads are not linear.

Order of percentage of referrals traded by dyad

Dyad		Dyad count	Referral count	% referrals traded
Close - Close	4-4	24	33	138%
Close - Aquaint	2-4	36	37	103%
Close - Friend	3-4	89	87	98%
Friend - No rel	3-1	32	20	63%
Friend - Aquaint	3-2	444	248	56%
Friend - Friend	3-3	210	111	53%

Figure 15. Order of percentages of referrals traded by dyad.

As Figure 15 demonstrates, close friend/close friend dyads returned a greater percentage of referrals. Furthermore, close friend/acquaintance, friend/no relationship and friend/acquaintance dyads all returned more referral results than did friend/friend dyads. This suggests that literature assumptions and definitions of relationship dyads that are grouped into only three categories do not account for a true picture of network relationship.

To analyze linear groupings for regression analysis, each dyad was scored based on the sum of the relationships as described in Figure 16. For example, the friend/acquaintance dyad resulted in a score of 5 because one member of a dyad identified the other as a friend (score 3) and the reciprocating dyad member identified the other as an acquaintance (score 2). Together, the total score for this friend/acquaintance dyad is 5. Furthermore, the difference between these two individual scores is 1, suggesting that there is one score measure between their mutual scores.

		1 No relationship	2 Acquaintance	3 Friend	4 Close friend
1	No relationship	1-1	1-2	1-3	1-4
	Sum of dyad score	2	3	4	5
	Delta from score	0	1	2	3
2	Acquaintance		2-2	2-3	2-4
	Sum of dyad score		4	5	6
	Delta from score		0	1	2
3	Friend			3-3	3-4
	Sum of dyad score			6	7
	Delta from score			0	1
4	Close friend				4-4
	Sum of dyad score				8
	Delta from score				0

Figure 16. Sum of dyad relationship scores and delta between each score for logistical regression.

Using logistic regression, relationship scores among all groups (Figure 16) were analyzed for linear combinations and significance of all possible predictor variables (Sheskin, 2004). This analysis is presented in Figure 17.

Ordinal Logistic Fit for Total Referals

Whole Model Test

Model	-LogLikelihood	DF	ChiSquare	Prob>ChiSq
Difference	57.5500	4	115.1	<.0001*
Full	1572.4344			
Reduced	1629.9844			

RSquare (U)	0.0353	
Observations (or Sum Wgts)	1845	

Converged by Gradient

Lack Of Fit

Source	DF	-LogLikelihood	ChiSquare
Lack Of Fit	41	15.6745	31.34905
Saturated	45	1556.7599	Prob>ChiSq
Fitted	4	1572.4344	0.8617

Parameter Estimates

Term	Estimate	Std Error	ChiSquare	Prob>ChiSq
Intercept[0]	0.63052361	0.134654	21.93	<.0001*
Intercept[1]	2.06652051	0.1461005	200.07	<.0001*
Intercept[2]	3.05082145	0.1726165	312.37	<.0001*
Intercept[3]	3.93413649	0.2221874	313.52	<.0001*
Intercept[4]	4.36570264	0.2596784	282.64	<.0001*
Intercept[5]	5.3760298	0.3969083	183.46	<.0001*
Intercept[6]	6.22806115	0.5899835	111.44	<.0001*
Intercept[7]	6.63490407	0.7175733	85.49	<.0001*
Intercept[8]	7.32914124	1.0075331	52.92	<.0001*
Total Relationship{2&3&4-5&6&7&8}	0.69399773	0.069768	98.95	<.0001*
Total Relationship{2&3-4}	0.48743517	0.1006921	23.43	<.0001*
Total Relationship{5&6-7&8}	0.41554698	0.0963967	18.58	<.0001*
Delta Relationship{0&1-2&3}	0.27111655	0.1215613	4.97	0.0257*

Effect Likelihood Ratio Tests

Source	Nparm	DF	L-R ChiSquare	Prob>ChiSq
Total Relationship{2&3&4-5&6&7&8}	1	1	101.193753	<.0001*
Total Relationship{2&3-4}	1	1	27.4627792	<.0001*
Total Relationship{5&6-7&8}	1	1	17.0285588	<.0001*
Delta Relationship{0&1-2&3}	1	1	4.36332231	0.0367*

Figure 17. Logistic regression - ordinal logistical fit of total relationships.

Logistical regression results demonstrated, with statistical significance, several differences between the groups. Specifically, strong-, weak- and no-relationship dyad groups did not adhere neatly to the group categories used in this study. Figure 18 highlights these differences.

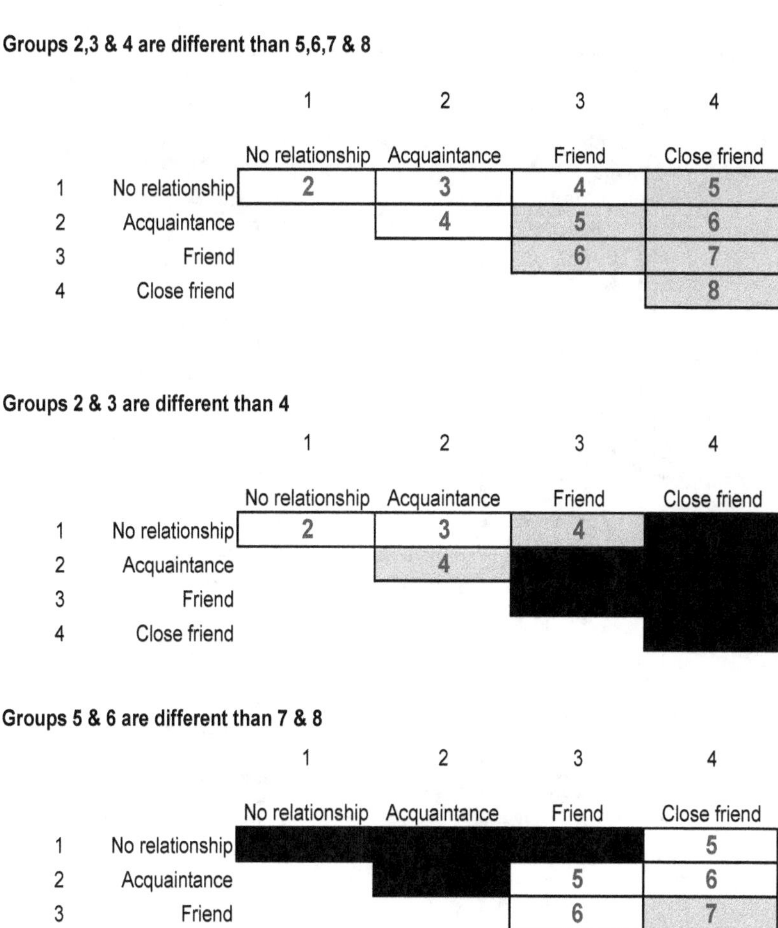

Figure 18. Differences in groups as a result of logistical regression.

Therefore, the relationship between variables is different than categorical groupings of tie strength suggested within the network literature. These results also represent that there is a variance between the deltas of scores for the dyad categories. Specifically, there is a difference between delta scores of 0 and 1 and 2 and 3. Therefore, the delta relationship between dyad scores presented in Figure 16 has an effect on referral giving. Figure 19 presents a logistical fit of all scores by total referrals traded.

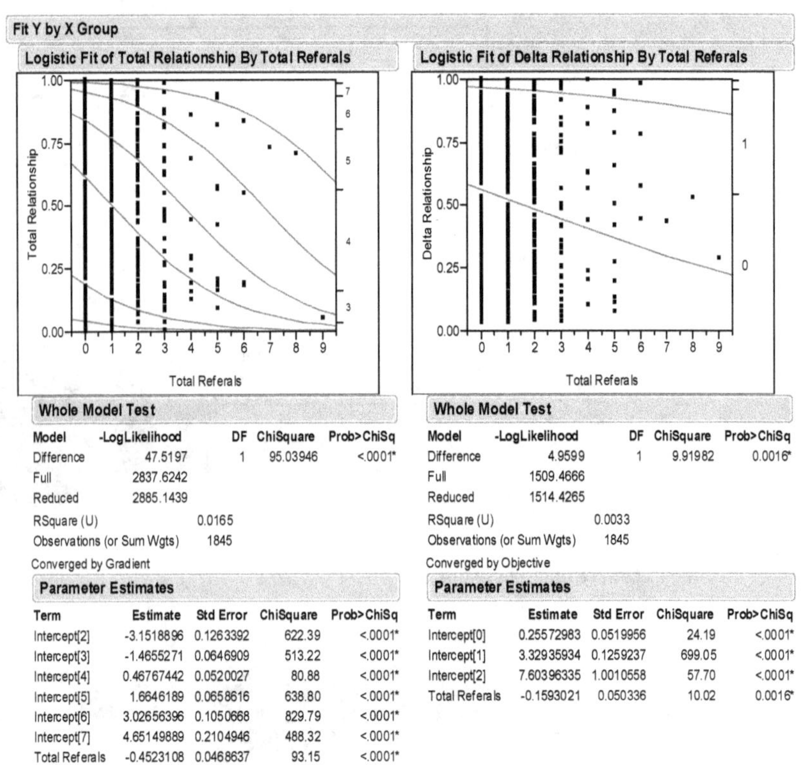

Logistic Fit of Total Relationship By Total Referals

Whole Model Test

Model	-LogLikelihood	DF	ChiSquare	Prob>ChiSq
Difference	47.5197	1	95.03946	<.0001*
Full	2837.6242			
Reduced	2885.1439			

RSquare (U)	0.0165
Observations (or Sum Wgts)	1845

Converged by Gradient

Parameter Estimates

Term	Estimate	Std Error	ChiSquare	Prob>ChiSq
Intercept[2]	-3.1518896	0.1263392	622.39	<.0001*
Intercept[3]	-1.4655271	0.0646909	513.22	<.0001*
Intercept[4]	0.46767442	0.0520027	80.88	<.0001*
Intercept[5]	1.6646189	0.0658616	638.80	<.0001*
Intercept[6]	3.02656396	0.1050668	829.79	<.0001*
Intercept[7]	4.65149889	0.2104946	488.32	<.0001*
Total Referals	-0.4523108	0.0468637	93.15	<.0001*

Logistic Fit of Delta Relationship By Total Referals

Whole Model Test

Model	-LogLikelihood	DF	ChiSquare	Prob>ChiSq
Difference	4.9599	1	9.91982	0.0016*
Full	1509.4666			
Reduced	1514.4265			

RSquare (U)	0.0033
Observations (or Sum Wgts)	1845

Converged by Objective

Parameter Estimates

Term	Estimate	Std Error	ChiSquare	Prob>ChiSq
Intercept[0]	0.25572983	0.0519956	24.19	<.0001*
Intercept[1]	3.32935934	0.1259237	699.05	<.0001*
Intercept[2]	7.60396335	1.0010558	57.70	<.0001*
Total Referals	-0.1593021	0.050336	10.02	0.0016*

Figure 19. Logistical fit of the total scores delta relationships to those scores of referrals traded.

These results present the finding that the further away (the delta) the relationship is from another dyad member, the higher percent of referrals those dyads provide to one another. Conversely, the closer the mutuality of the dyad relationship is, the lower percentage of referrals is likely to be traded.

To further illustrate the effect of the dyad groupings and the resulting delta among each grouping, a linear regression of the data is explored. While linear regression requires continuous predictor variable data to be relevant, it does provide a visual representation of this study's results (Sheskin, 2004). Figure 20 presents a contour plot for total referrals by group (total relationship of a dyad) and delta relationships among each group.

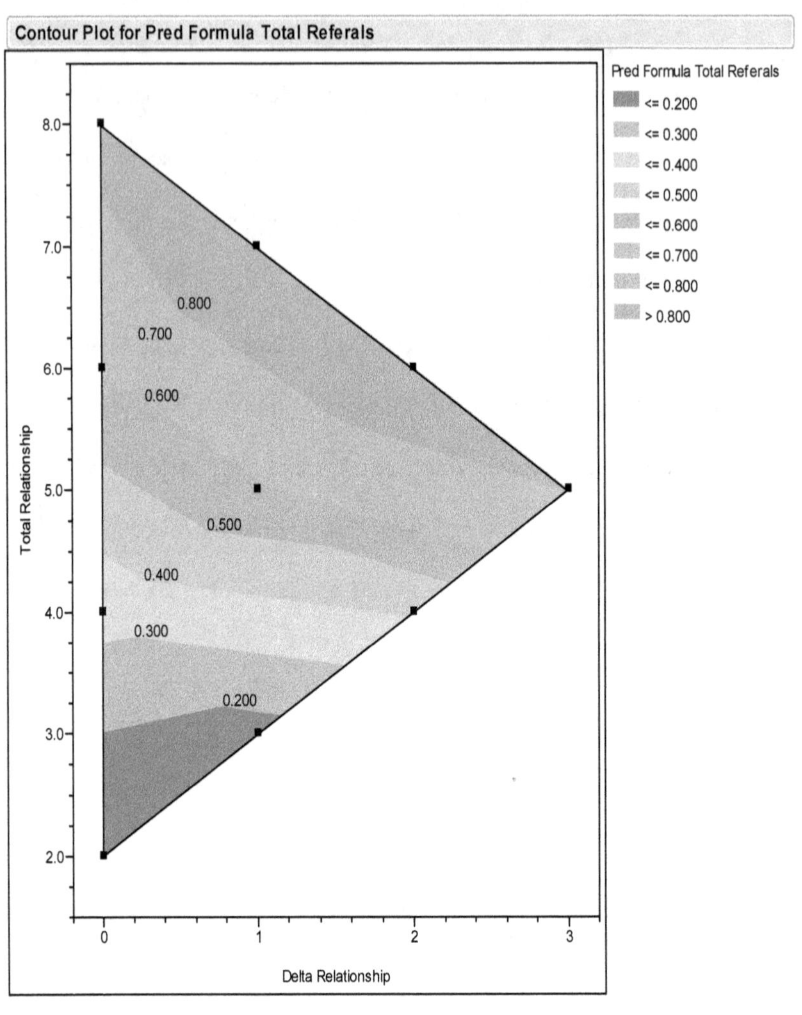

Figure 20. Linear regression contour plot for total referrals by group and delta

relationships among each group.

This contour plot demonstrates that relationship strength does not predict a linear referral

yield among dyads. Total dyad relationships, which score approximately between 4 and

7, produce different referral yield based on the difference between the relationships. For example, a dyad score of 6 represents both friend/friend (3+3=6, delta of 0) and close friend/acquaintance (4+2=6, delta of 2). Using these scores, friend/friend dyads only produced on average .7 referrals while a close friend/acquaintance dyad produced .8 referrals per dyad. This delta effect suggests that many of the friendship dyads established within the literature and in this study are not good predictors of results.

Research Question and Hypothesis Results

The research question in this study was: Is there an association between relationship tie-strength and goal-directed outcomes for members of structured networking goal-directed organizations? The fundamental hypotheses established in this study was that relationship strength and referral trading output possess a positive relationship that is statistically significant. Moreover, the nature of a dyad relationship, being strong, weak, or nonexistent, would have a positive effect on the referral results people experience.

The preceding analysis warrants that the null hypothesis not be rejected. Therefore, the alternative hypothesis that there is a difference ($p<.05$) between tie-strength and referral outcome for members of a goal-directed networking group is rejected. While these results do suggest there are differences, the result between strong- and weak-tie relationships only achieved a significance of $p<.0972$. There is not sufficient evidence to support the prediction that a strong or weak tie can predict referral outcome. In addition, logistic regression analysis demonstrates with significance that categories of dyad grouping affect referral result. Additionally, the distance between relationships for dyad members, rather than the closeness of them, will increase the economic return of referrals. This research study failed to reject the null hypothesis:

There is no difference (P>.05) between tie-strength and referral outcome of members of a goal-directed networking group.

Summary

Chapter 4 described the results of network adjacency matrix analysis (tie-strength), content analysis (referrals traded) and the statistical methods applied to these variables. The Kruskal-Wallis one-way analysis of variance by rank was applied to the variables to determine statistical significance between the variable results. Additionally, logistic regression of the variables was applied for more refined analysis. This chapter presented a review of the research procedure and methodology, and described the results in the context of the research question and hypothesis that underlay this study. Furthermore, conclusions were drawn regarding the statistical significance of relationship strength in predicting referral results for network actors.

Relationship tie-strength data from 184 individuals (n=184) was collected from 10 BNI groups in the greater Manchester New Hampshire area. This data produced relationship dyad counts for strong-, weak- and no-tie relationship groups. As a result, 3,692 relationship measures to other group members and 1,846 dyad relationships were accounted for in this research. Referrals traded (822 referrals) among the dyads were collected and accounted for to compare and correlate to dyad strength.

The primary objective of this research study was to determine if there is a correlation between relationship tie-strength and goal-directed outcomes for members of structured networking goal-directed organizations. The result of statistical tests warrants that the null hypothesis not be rejected. Therefore, the alternative hypothesis that there is a relationship ($p<.05$) between tie-strength and referral outcome for members of a goal-directed networking group is rejected. While these results do suggest there are differences, the result between strong- and weak-tie relationships only achieved a significance of $p<.0972$. There is not sufficient evidence to support the prediction that a strong or weak tie can predict referral outcome. In addition, logistic regression analysis demonstrates with significance that categories of dyad grouping affect referral result. Additionally, the distance between relationships for dyad members, rather than the closeness of them, will increase the economic return of referrals.

Chapter 5 summarizes this research study's results, considers possible implications for network actors and organizations, and suggests recommendations for future research. The possible implications for leaders who require networks of people and possible intervention for goal-directed groups are explored.

CHAPTER 5: SUMMARY AND RECOMMENDATIONS

The purpose of the present quantitative correlation research study was to determine the relationship between goal-directed network membership relationship strength (tie-strength) and the goal-results these relationships yield. Tie-strength was determined through simple network analysis, creating a clear delineation between strong, weak, and null tie affiliations among the goal-directed sample members (Scott, 2003). Goal-results were measured through analysis of referral development result records accumulated by the goal-directed organization. This analysis was performed on a sample of 184 (n=184) Business Networking International (BNI) members in New Hampshire who are affiliated for the purposes of business development through relationship building and referral sharing. This study examined the usefulness of tie-strength in relation to business referral results, and the value of tie development in a goal-directed network group.

The predictor variable in this quantitative study was the tie-strength of the members within a goal-directed networking group, as determined using network adjacency matrix analysis to produce asymmetric data (Kilduff & Tsai, 2006). The criterion variable was the volume of referrals produced through member goal-directed behavior.

This study's focal point was the association between network member relationship strength (tie strength) and the economic utility these relationships yielded in the context of goal-directed networking activity. This chapter presents a summary of this study's purpose, results, implications and future research recommendations. Possible explanations for the unexpected findings this study produced are also explored with associated implications for future research and organizational leadership.

Problem, Purpose, and Methodology

The problem investigated was detailed in Chapter 1 and the relevant literature was presented in Chapter 2. Chapter 3 presented the methodology and application of this research. Chapter 4 presented detail statistical results to answer the research question and associated findings. To place these results in the context of this research study, the problem, purpose and methodology is reviewed here.

Problem

The literature review in this study identified changes in networking practices and structures within contemporary organizational contexts. Specifically, relationship networks have shifted from civic to professional communities (Putnam, 2000). Further globalization, technology access, an organizational team orientation, and the growth of small business support the likelihood that new networking methods and behaviors are being deployed and used (Parkhe, Wasserman & Ralston, 2006). While networks can be mapped within an organization or community, and used by the organizational actors and entrepreneurs to find information, resources, and access, they neither are accounted for nor measured in any tangible way (Badaracco, 2002). Networking must be conceptualized in the mind of the actor and executed in a rational way. Any prescription of a networking practice depends on the context, situation, and the individual personality of the participant. For networking behavior and its possible value to an individual or organization to be realized, there must exist purposeful strategy and execution of action. It is human nature to be social, to network with one another, and important to any organizational construct (Parkhe et al., 2006). Yet the complexities of network structure and behavior are beyond any universal rule or law. If a leader or network practitioner socially engages with the wrong individuals in pursuit of a goal, opportunities may be lost. Therefore, leaders, organizations, and individuals must carefully select, activate, and manage their social network activities for results, or waste valuable time, energy, and money in the pursuit of any performance advantage. This research examined productive network dyad results within the contexts of these structural and social changes to add insight for network actors regarding economic utility of networking relationship behavior.

The establishment of relationships through networking practices can produce economic value. A network actor's primary method to produce network results is through the development of varying degrees of dyad relationships with other network actors. These relationships can be strong, weak, or not advance beyond an initial introduction. This research examined the productive results of each relationship that can be established among dyads of network actors.

Parkhe, Wasserman, and Ralston (2006) recognize the current macro shifts in organizational context and believe future research of network productivity can improve business success. However, if the network research merely analyzes complicated mathematical models and maps, understanding of organizational behavior may be missed and ways to apply successful methods will remain unknown. Therefore, to advance the theoretical knowledge of networks, practical understanding of outcomes for these theories within time and space (contextual) are important. In addition, the utility and economic results derived from time and space may provide predictive application for similar networking groups. This research informs leaders and professionals about utility and economic value based on a contemporary structure and the relationship practices of networking in a contemporary organizational situation

Purpose

The purpose of this study was to determine to what degree networking relationship tie-strength affects referral exchange results (utility) among members of a referral exchange goal-directed networking group in New Hampshire. The predictor variable (tie-strength) was measured through network adjacency matrix analysis to determine weak-tie and strong-tie relationship dyads (Kilduff & Tsai, 2006). The criterion variable (results) was measured through content analysis of referral result data maintained by the group. These results provided insight into the economic utility of each dyad relationship for correlational analysis. Intervening variables were also collected, including frequency of member one-on-one meetings outside the group's formal meeting, frequency of attendance of group training provided by the organization, time within profession, and length of group affiliation.

This study provides actors within goal-directed network groups, leaders, and organizational participants who actively use networking for productive purposes insight into economic utility and value for their efforts. In addition, this study offers insight to scholars about networking and relationship behavior important to advancing interpersonal productivity and intervention.

The present research considered the impact of relationship strength in the context and construct of goal-directed networking groups. The following research question is reflective of this study's framework and purpose: Is there an association between relationship tie-strength and goal-directed outcomes for members of structured networking goal-directed organizations? The fundamental alternative hypothesis established in this study was that relationship strength and referral trading output possess a positive relationship that is statistically significant. Moreover, the nature of a dyad relationship, being strong, weak, or nonexistent, would have an effect on the referral results people experience.

Methodology

This study examined the dyad relationships and referral trading results for the membership of 10 BNI groups in the greater Manchester New Hampshire area. To determine dyad relationship strength (predictor variable), network adjacency matrix analysis was used. This method is a relational data-sorting procedure used in social network analysis (Scott, 2003). The results of this method compared mutual relationships that were linked and the associated strength of those relationships. Referral trading among the dyads (criterion variable) was determined through a content analysis of documented referral results that were collected by each group.

Data was successfully collected from 10 of the 12 targeted BNI groups during the month of September 2007. One group withdrew from the study 2 weeks prior to data collection and one group disbanded the week of data collection. The 10 groups that did participate in this study had a total target sample population of 239 members, of which 184 (n=184) participated and completed the survey. Therefore, the sample response rate was 77% from the total sample populations. Most members who did not participate were absent the day of the survey. Of the surveys collected, only 4 were removed from the study's results because they were not complete. Because this study used network adjacency matrix analysis to determine dyad relationships, all the relationship data collected for the members who were not present at the time of survey, or did not complete the survey, were removed. The data that remains in the analysis is only for intact identified dyad relationships.

Content data for the referrals of all participants traded for the 3 month sample frame (June through August 2007) was collected from each group's vice-president at the time the survey was administered.

The statistical test used in this study to satisfy the research question and hypothesis was the Kruskal-Wallis one-way analysis of variance by rank, a nonparametric test used when data is ordinal (Sheskin, 2004). The Kruskal-Wallis test reduces the impact of outliers by ranking the data. The Kruskal-Wallis one-way analysis of variance by rank was applied to all three variable groups (tie-strength), and refined further to determine the statistical significance between strong- and weak-tie groups.

This study also employed logistical regression to refine the results obtained by the Kruskal-Wallis one-way analysis of the variance by rank. Logistical regression is a multivariate statistic used to produce linear combinations of predictor variables (Sheskin, 2004). Because the Kruskal-Wallis test produced unforeseen results, it was necessary to further analyze tie strength dyad relationships' effect on the criterion variable. Specifically, logistical regression allowed for a statistical explanation for failing to reject the null hypothesis.

Statistical Results

The Kruskal-Wallis one-way analysis of the variance applied to all variables proved that there are different yields of referrals for people with varying relationships.

The percentage of referrals traded using a one-way perspective (one person's friendship perspective of another) suggests that a network actor is more likely to give a higher percentage of referrals based on a one-way friendship strength perspective. Therefore, those who are considered a stronger friend to someone receive a higher percentage of referrals. Using the Kruskal-Wallis one-way analysis of the variance for all groups validates that this difference is significant (Chi Square <.0001). When data is matched and grouped into dyads for comparison (strong, weak, and no relationship), strong-tie relationships also appear to receive more referrals than those dyad relationships that are weaker. Therefore, based on the analyses of all dyad groups, the data suggests that there are significant differences among at least two possible dyad and one-way relationship perspectives (Sheskin, 2004).

To refine understanding of these whole group significance tests, all possible combinations of groups were tested against one another using the Kruskal-Wallis test. These results indicate that perceived close friends received more referrals than friends, friends more than acquaintances and acquaintances more than no relationship. All possible combination tests demonstrated with significance (Chi Square <.0001) that a one-way relationship perspective can predict a greater level of referral trading utility.

When applying the Kruskal-Wallis test to relationship dyad combinations, the results were less consistent than the one-way relationship test. Specifically, when comparing weak-tie to strong-tie dyads using the Kruskal-Wallis test, this study found the result to not be significant at a < .05 level. These results suggest a contradiction between one-way relationship referral giving and dyad referral giving. From a one-way perspective, one person's friendship perspective of another, results in more referrals received for the person who is perceived as a friend. Dyad relationship where there is mutual reciprocation of that friendship perspective did not result in more referrals traded to these dyad members. Therefore, this study failed to reject the null hypothesis that there is no difference between tie-strength and referral outcome of members of a goal-directed networking group. However, there are statistically significant results to suggest that what one person perceives the relationship to be will result in a referral receiving outcome.

Because the Kruskal-Wallis tests produced contradicting results between the one-way and dyad comparisons, logistical regression was used to determine linear combinations of the predictor variables (Sheskin, 2004). Specifically, the logistical regression allowed for a statistical explanation for failing to reject the null hypotheses.

Logistical regression was applied to 10 dyad group possibilities, further refining the three categories originally defined for this study (strong, weak, and no relationship). When analyzing all 10 groups separately, anomalies in the dyad data emerged. Specifically, several weak-tie relationship dyads traded more referrals than did mutual friendship relationship (strong-tie relationship). This suggests that literature assumptions and definitions of relationship dyads that are grouped into only three categories do not account for a true depiction of network relationships. Additionally, the further the relationship distance between the members of a dyad is from another dyad member, the higher the percent of referrals those dyads provide to one another. Conversely, the closer the mutuality of the dyad relationship, the lower the percentage of referrals traded is.

Findings and Implications

The value of network research is to discover and interpret unobvious potential and illuminate obstacles of human connections (Kilduff & Tsai, 2006). Social principles and properties can be used to improve productivity, strategy, and results, or reduce limitations of personal actor capacity. This study supports previous relationship theory while offering a deeper understanding of intrinsic motivation and behavior at the dyad level. In addition, these findings provide insight into how social behavior may be managed for better results.

This research study failed to reject the null hypothesis; yet dyad relationship complexity within social networks is illuminated for reflection on previous research and adds a greater understanding of network relationship behavior. It is concluded that weak-tie relationships are important for gaining information, reaching other networks, and finding structural holes that can lead to better network results. Additionally, dyad relationship interactions support the structural properties of network development by providing the initial motivation for people to reach outside their already held friendship spheres.

An unintended finding of this research is that relationship perspectives people hold for one another tend to effect their motivation to extend economic value. As illustrated in Figure 21, the further away a relationship is from symmetry (agreement of a relationship perspective), the higher the percentage of referrals traded is. Most interesting is that these referrals were traded one-way towards the person who reported having a lesser relationship.

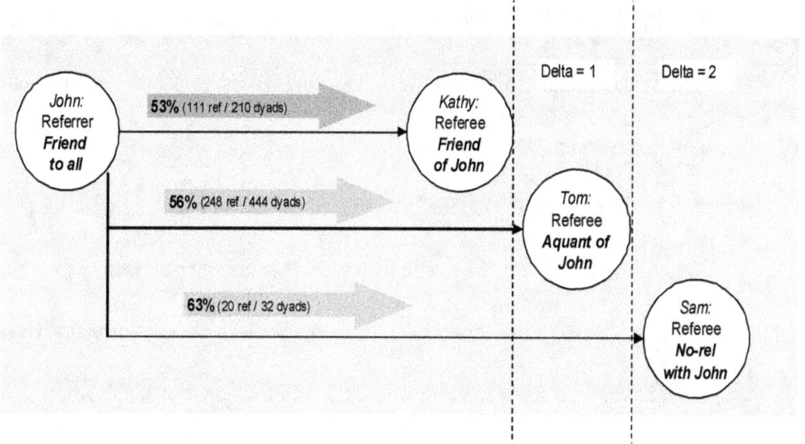

Figure 21. Non-symmetry of referral results.

The greater the distance of asymmetry (delta perception within the dyad) is, the more referrals are traded. Therefore, based on these results, the greatest economic value comes from one being a perceived friend rather than a true one. Whether this phenomenon is conscious or unconscious on the part of the actors is beyond the scope of this study. However, cognitive balance theory is explored for a possible explanation.

The following section will review this study's findings in the context of previous social network theory, and explore possible implications for leaders and organizational participants.

Weak-Tie Theory

Empirical findings support the perspective that varying levels of relationship tie strength hold varying economic value (Ibarra, Kilduff & Tsai, 2005). Granovetter's (1973) analysis of the value of dyadic ties suggests that weak-ties (within a network) contribute significantly to bridging small groups, thereby yielding networking results. Specifically, weaker relationships provide access to networks that are new. By reaching into weaker relationships, a network actor finds access to people, information, and possible economic value.

Granovetter (1973, 1983) concluded two major benefits for his weak-tie theory. Weak-ties provide utility because they provide longer range (reach) potential to distant information and offer economy due to shorter paths to direct information (breadth). If an actor has at least a few weak-ties, access to information is available, even if that information has to travel a longer path. Additionally, if an actor has many weak-tie relationships, there is a likelihood of receiving more information. In a labor market study of job attainment, Granovetter (1973) determined tie-strength relationships based on frequency of interaction. He concluded that most people found job positions (results) from people they only had occasional contact with. The least job positions found came from people who reported having contact often with others who provided them the job information. Therefore, he concluded that most people received job attainment information from those relationships that are weaker based on the frequency of interaction.

While Granovetter's (1973) research considered dyadic ties, these ties were not mutually validated. He only asked job seekers the strength of their relationships (based on frequency of contact). Therefore, his research only considered a one-way perspective in determining relationship strength, and that perspective was for those who were the receivers of information. The present research study found a similar result when looking at one way data from receivers of information (referrals traded). Specifically, those who perceived their relationship with a giver as weaker within a dyad relationship received more information. Conversely, those who considered their relationship stronger in a dyad relationship received less information. Therefore, when considering one-way relationship information and the results it yields, this study validates Granovetter's findings. However, Granovetter's conclusion that the skew of results to the weak end of the relationship is due to structure rather than motivation is not supported by the present research.

The present research study considered mutual dyad relationships, which provides additional insight into dyad motivation. The mutual dyad perspective in the present study illuminates varying results based on the relationship construction (dyad) rather than the structural construction (reach) of the network. It seems that people who are perceived as friends, although the perception is not shared with a dyad partner, have an advantage over those who are in fact mutual friends. Personal motivation and perspective has a cooperative effect with structural properties of extending a network. Structural bridges provided by weak-ties are initially affected by dyad motivation. Therefore, because people tend to provide results (referral information) to those who do not share their perspective in relationship, the network is naturally extended (bridged) to other network contacts. This cooperation between personal motivation to provide to those with an incomplete relationship and the structural properties of bridges that Granovetter (1973, 1983) recognized provides the properties for social connections to travel. If people only provided mutual friends information or results, no bridges would be developed and people would only find value in cliques, which is not productive. Therefore, motivation, conscious or unconscious, is an important property for extending social networks.

In Granovetter's (1973) research, he acknowledged that tie strength for a dyad should be represented by a combination of variables: amount of time, emotional intensity, intimacy and reciprocal services provided to one another. His research only examined frequency (amount of time) of interaction and reciprocal services. The present research study benefits from the construct of the BNI procedures to account for frequency and reciprocal services and adds the perspective of intimacy and emotional intensity by examining the reciprocal perspective of friendship perception. Granovetter (1973) acknowledged the value of mutual choice of friendship, but made assumptions about this choice based on a frequency response from those receiving service. The present study found that neatly placing relationships into categories of strong, weak, and no relationship limits the results. In this study, regression analysis of 10 possible dyad relationship categories determined that relationships are more complicated. Specifically, some dyad relationships in the present study found one relationship perspective to be that of friends, and the other perspective that no relationship existed, yet their collective results were more than those of mutual friends. Therefore, the present study provides more visibility into the complexities of dyad strength and the complementary intensity of relationship.

While this study supports Granovetter's (1973, 1983) conclusions that weak-ties bridge information between weaker relationship dyads, it may have more to do with the complexity of mutual relationship than network reach utility. Cognitive motivation to provide for certain people over others is not visible from the structural perspective that Granovetter's theory implies. Weak-ties are structurally important, and it is logical that information travels through them, but the motivation for information to travel through these structures may be unconscious to the network actor. This motivation may be an instinct or a reflex to act productively in a social network arrangement. Granovetter stated, the "…removal of the average weak tie would do more 'damage' to transmission probabilities than would that of the average strong one" (p. 1366). This is true, but for more than network structural reasons.

Structural Holes Theory

Structural holes are disconnections within a network that offer network actors opportunities (Burt, 1992). The structural hole theory is one of entrepreneurial freedom in a competitive environment that is negotiated, not developed, held or controlled. Burt argues that structural holes have little to do with player attributes or the results of activities. Rather, structural hole opportunities are attributes of player relations and the process of competition. Structural holes are invisible and act as barriers to information flow. In addition, these invisible network properties are sought blindly in the act of competing. Burt recognizes that these holes are relational, not physical, and require interaction for opportunities to be realized. He further recognizes that solving these network puzzles is a human behavior attribute, not a physical or structural attribute. Therefore, to extend Granovetter's (1973, 1983) ideas about structural reach there is a recognition that invisible human properties are at work that can advance or limit results of social behavior.

While relationship development is critical, Burt (1992) is clear that people are the vehicles of action, not the source of it. The source of action, he argues, is the structure, connections, and holes. He argues that people are improvisational, behaving within the structure of a physical network that has physical rules. However, if people are making decisions purposely or un-purposely detached from the physical rules, they are the source of the next network link. If a person is proactively providing for another who he considers a friend, yet is unconsciously aware that the receiving person feels very different about that relationship, how does the giver know he is bridging a network or probing a structural hole? The present research suggests that somehow the giver may be unconsciously aware that he is changing the properties of his relationship and network and seeking bridges and structural holes. Furthermore, even a network that is considered dense and having equivalency can produce structural holes because what appears to be dense and equivalent may not be.

It is logical that the less dense a network is, and the less equivalent it is, the more opportunities network actors have to discover structural holes and produce bridges and opportunities. However, some network actors appear to be making decisions, improvisationally, about which relationship requires action. It is possible that people tend to fulfill unconsciously perceived asymmetric relationships with actions that may lead to opportunity that is not visible. This tendency also may be a relationship competitive strategy to secure productive relationships that Burt (1992) recognized. What Burt describes as improvisational may really be a natural tendency to complete relationships that are unconsciously perceived as incomplete.

Organizational Politics

Politics, as a tool, may be considered as negative for the organization and its actors. Negative aspects of political behavior can be career debilitating and potentially destructive; however, it is part of the human condition. "It may be claimed that OP [organizational politics] is an aspect of organizational behavior so deeply rooted in human nature and in the basic organizational setup that its negative implications can never be entirely eliminated" (Drory, 1993, p. 75). The claim that political behaviors are a natural phenomenon is somewhat validated in the present research study. These results demonstrate that people are behaving naturally, with some unconscious purpose, to gain access to information and networks by favoring certain dyad relationship arrangements. The second claim Drory makes, that political behavior cannot be removed from the social environment, also has merit. If people are behaving instinctually towards developing relationships of value, without cognitive awareness, it is harder to control through organizational structure. Therefore, structural design may benefit from leveraging the instinct to expand relationships and information through forums that allow political behavior to be productively used.

Quantitative research results suggest that the perception of the use of political behavior is negative to those who do not possess the skills to use it (Harrell-Cook, Ferris, & Dulebohn, 1999). Research also demonstrates that the network behaviors to produce structural bridges and holes also have advantages (Granovetter, 1973, 1983, Burt, 1992). In addition, the present research suggests that when participating in networking activities, people may be naturally enacting relationships for advantage. Those with a negative perception of politics are likely to have little control of their environment and miss many opportunities from which they would otherwise benefit. Therefore, those who refuse to engage in social networking as a personal value choice may be at an organizational disadvantage.

Reciprocity and Exchange Theory

Reciprocity is considered an important networking property that requires balance of exchange among participants (Cohan, & Bradford, 1989). Therefore, providing information, favors or referrals to another person produces an expectation of a return at some future date. This concept can be applied to a contract of trade or an implied trade. Yet the results in this research study indicate that reciprocity has something to do with relationship properties in addition to tangible currency.

Cohan and Bradford (1989) suggested steps to engage reciprocity: See a target, find a need, know the value of the need, and understand exchange as a concept. This assumes awareness, when what may be happening is instinctual. There may be no need for actors to understand reciprocity beyond "we're here to trade," and then it is instinctual, and purposeful acts are less important than building a perspective of a person. Cohan and Bradford (1989) suggest the importance of understanding exchange and its role. If exchange is not understood or embraced as a useful tool, it will not be enacted. While it may be important for people to understand exchange as an important activity, it is also important that they understand that there are natural tendencies for people to be attracted to certain other people to productively exchange with. This research supports the idea that natural human behavior is affecting the exchange process.

In this study's results, network actors who did not have completed friendship relationships tended to provide currency in the form of referrals. Cohan and Bradford (1989) describe commonly traded organizational currencies as tangible and intangible. Intangible currencies include acceptance, support, and improved concept of self. Therefore, network actors may sense the availability of these intangible currencies and act to receive them by providing tangible currencies like referrals. In addition, people may perceive a gap or lack of these currencies and act to close the gap that is perceived. Regardless of the currency traded, reciprocal patterns in this study are not balanced among the network participants.

In an exchange relationship, two theories should be considered (Alessio, 1990). Exchange theory considers the balance of exchange between people, tangible and intangible. Balance theory is related to exchange theory because exchange can affect balance within a dyad. Since exchange is not formally measured, it becomes a cognitive process of informal accounting that is cumulative and can create balance or imbalance. An imbalance can motivate people to take action to find balance. The next section discusses the process of cognitive balance.

Cognitive Balance Theory

Heider's balance theory recognizes the natural need of people to find balance in compatibility, consistency or harmony (Willis & Burgess, 1974). Stability is achieved when harmony between people is balanced and instable when harmony is not balanced. Eventually, imbalance produces tension that can result in taking action to produce a balanced state. When a dyad is in balance, stress is absent and change is not motivated (Woodside, & Chebat, 2001). Balance is also dependent on the dyad perception, not a one-way perception. This balance and imbalance and resulting motivation to act (provide referrals within unbalanced dyads) was found in the present study. Specifically, network dyads that were out of perceptual balance took more referral trading action than those dyads in balance.

Unbalanced situations stimulate us to further thinking; they have the

character of interesting puzzles, problems which make us suspect a depth

of interesting background. . . . Stories in which the stress is laid on

unbalanced situations are felt to have a deep psychological meaning.

(Heider in Woodside & Chebat, 2001)

For an action to be motivated within a relationship dyad, an evolution of conscious or

unconscious cognition can occur. Borrowing from Woodside and Chebat's (2001)

explanation of how imbalance returns to balance, the following three steps are

considered. First, dyad actors become aware of each other. Then, controlled thinking of

the other person and a perception of a relationship imbalance occur. Finally, an actor

takes cognitive and behavioral action to reduce the tension and realize relationship

balance again. In the present study, the actor who perceived the imbalance may be acting

on the relationship perception and attempting to relieve tension in the dyad relationship.

The implication of this possible cognitive balance result within the present study

is that individuals who network may be in a constant state of seeking balance among

members of their network. This possible natural inclination supports structural network

properties and naturally extends networks beyond cliques. Therefore, if network actors

possess an understanding of this natural inclination, they may be able to better recognize

imbalance to seek structural holes within their networks. Furthermore, it may be better to

hold more perceived imbalanced relationships where others are seeking to find the

balance, thereby providing more information and access to opportunities.

While most of the initial literature on balance theory focused on balance within

triad relationships, subsequent studies consider the same theory for dyads (Willis &

Burgess, 1974). There are multiple variables that may cause imbalance, which is beyond the scope of this research. This research examined friendship strength as a variable. Yet it is likely that power, personality, trust or the many possible relational currencies that people can perceive may have an impact on producing motivation for cognitive balance. In addition, any of the possible exchange currencies that Cohan and Bradford (1989) proposed may also affect balance outcomes.

Leadership Implications

Leadership is a social construct requiring people to perceive each other in a way that will produce collective behavior. A fundamental message of transformational leadership is that serving others is more important than serving oneself (Bass, 1990). Transformational leadership requires a social perspective and commitment. This perspective can be large, including the whole society itself, or as small as every interaction between individuals. Leadership finds utility in every relationship formed. Therefore, networking activities and behaviors facilitate the ability to reach people at a distance and produce relationships that will motivate people to act. Networking and its inherent relationship value is a critical component to advancing the activities of leadership practices.

Transformational leadership practices support the organizing shift to flatter, transparent, and empowered work arrangements. This requires a shift to using influence without authority across individuals, functions, companies and industries. Therefore, social capital is of increasing importance for individuals to develop referent power and trust. These attributes are not written on an organizational chart, and individual contributors are left to their own devices to develop and practice new relationship behaviors. This shift towards decentralization and empowerment requires organizational contributors to behave more independently while using team concepts to advance collective goals. Modern organization and leadership requires people to interact more to yield results. People must think as a team while still acting individually to find the resources they need to contribute value to the team. Networking provides the vehicle for people to reach across and outside an organization to find resources for information and action. As Granovetter (1973, 1983) and Burt (1992) have suggested, network structural properties aid those with less dense networks to find bridges to other networks and opportunities. Burt (1992) suggested that people are the vehicles of action, not the source of it. The implication of the present research is that people may be the sources of initial behavior that allows structural network properties to be realized for advantage. Therefore, individual actor behavior ultimately impacts leadership effect.

Leaders can directly benefit from networking properties and behaviors. In a study of Chief Executive Officers (CEOs) it was found that those leaders who sought advice from only their close contacts were at a decision-making disadvantage (McDonald & Westphal, 2003). Leaders who extended their networks beyond those they had immediate access to realized better strategic outcomes. Therefore, leaders themselves may find benefit from an understanding of network structural properties and cognitive balance principles. A leader who is aware of his relationship balance with others may be able to better identify structural bridges and holes, ultimately finding more information that will impact his decision making. Furthermore, leaders who support their direct reports in developing their own extended networks may realize more information and opportunities for the organization.

Since a primary leadership tenet is relationship, any means to advance a relationship perspective is beneficial. Formal structure does provide a means for leaders to communicate and build a perspective of themselves, and informal structures like networks provide additional benefits. In addition, further decentralizing of organizational strategies and practices places more importance on individual network behaviors. Networks provide structural advantage and weaker unbalanced relationships provide the motivation for people to provide exchange to close the balance gap. Therefore, leaders may benefit from managing their awareness of their structural networks and the relationships they contain. Not taking advantage of network understanding and relationship awareness places leaders and organizational actors at a disadvantage.

Allowing all organizational actors the same advantages of network awareness and benefits may improve organizational culture, productivity, and overall performance results. Creating goal-directed groups for the purposes of closing the cognitive balance gaps may produce exchange beyond serendipitous means. Rather than leaving networking activities to those who intuitively accept the value of creating and maintaining a network, leaders can create forums for people to reach across and outside organizations for value.

Some leaders and organizational actors may perceive networking activities as political or disruptive to traditional hierarchical and authoritative organizational cultures. For example, leaders who have realized success in older organizational paradigms built on hierarchical control may consider it risky for their executives to network outside their function. Their employees may find job opportunities that will negatively affect the leader's purpose. This fear is likely justified, yet limits the true reach and opportunity potential that is available outside one own firm. These transactional leadership perspectives may be jeopardizing an organization's full potential in a transformational business environment

Transformational leaders have a clear understanding that they cannot do it alone and leverage their followers to fulfill their mission. They embrace empowerment and trust as tools to execute change, and therefore require the ability to connect with people, trust them, and produce commitment. Bass (1999) believes these leaders "empower their followers by developing them into high involvement individuals and teams focused on quality, service, cost-effectiveness, and quantity of output of production" (p. 9). While a transactional leader may see this as loss of control, the transformational leader believes that a flatter organization is needed to create fundamental change (Bass, 1999). This implies that freedom of thought and all its value requires freedom of association. Therefore, networks and the relationships embedded within them provide value to a leader and the firm's mission.

Future Research Recommendations

The purpose of this quantitative correlation research study was to determine to what degree networking relationship tie-strength affects referral exchange results (utility) among members of a referral exchange goal-directed networking group in New Hampshire. The predictor variable (tie-strength) was measured through network adjacency matrix analysis to determine weak-tie and strong-tie relationship dyads (Kilduff & Tsai, 2006). The criterion variable (results) was measured through content analysis of referral result data maintained by the group.

This research considered the impact of relationship strength in the context and construct of goal-directed networking groups. The research question sought to determine if there is a correlation between relationship tie-strength and goal-directed outcomes for members of structured networking goal-directed organizations. The fundamental alternative hypothesis established in this study was that relationship strength and referral trading output possess a positive relationship that is statistically significant. Moreover, the nature of a dyad relationship, being strong, weak, or nonexistent, would have an effect on the referral results people experience.

This study failed to reject the null hypothesis that there is no difference between tie strength and referral outcome of members of a goal-directed networking group. However, there are statistically significant results to suggest that what one person perceives the relationship to be will result in a referral receiving outcome. Specifically, several weak-tie relationship dyads traded more referrals than did mutual friendship relationship (strong-tie relationship) dyads. This suggests that literature assumptions and definitions of relationship dyads that are grouped into only three categories do not account for a true depiction of network relationships. Additionally, the further the relationship distance between the members of a dyad relationship is from another dyad member, the higher percent of referrals those dyads provide to one another. Conversely, the closer the mutuality of the dyad relationships is, the lower the percentage of referrals likely to be traded is.

Future research regarding network relationship strength, delta effect of relationships, and possible cognitive balance should be broadened to include other contexts, constructs and variables. This research analyzed one goal-directed group that